Choose Love

STORMIE OMARTIAN

HARVEST HOUSE PUBLISHERS
EUGENE, OREGON

CHOOSE LOVE
Copyright © 2014 by Stormie Omartian
Published by Harvest House Publishers
Eugene, Oregon 97402
www.harvesthousepublishers.com

Library of Congress Cataloging-in-Publication Data
Omartian, Stormie.
Choose love / Stormie Omartian.
    pages cm
ISBN 978-0-7369-5897-4 (pbk.)
ISBN 978-0-7369-5898-1 (eBook)
1. God (Christianity)—Love. 2. God (Christianity)—Worship and love. 3. Love—Religious aspects—Christianity. I. Title.
BT140.O48 2014
231'.6—dc23

                                                            2014017271

Printed in the United States of America

14 15 16 17 18 19 20 21 22 / BP-JH / 10 9 8 7 6 5 4 3 2 1

*"You shall love the L*ORD *your God*
with all your heart, with all your soul,
with your entire mind, and with all your strength."
This is the first commandment.
And the second, like it, is this:
"You shall love your neighbor as yourself."
There is no other commandment greater than these.

MARK 12:30-31

Contents

First Choice

~~~~~~

Choose
to Receive
God's
Love
for You

1

See Yourself the Way
God Sees You

~~~~~~

I will never forget the day I first looked in one of those lighted magnifying mirrors. You know, the ones you can buy for your bathroom counter? They come in different levels of magnification. The one I bought was five times magnification because I needed to see certain things on my face and skin more clearly for the sake of good grooming.

I set it up, turned on the light, looked in the mirror, and nearly frightened myself to death.

I am warning you now that this is not for the faint of heart and you must prepare yourself in advance. First of all, be assured *before* you look in it that no one on earth sees you the way the mirror is reflecting you, with every pore and blemish enlarged; every brown sunspot, broken capillary, wrinkle, and line enhanced; and each imperfection—many of which you never even knew were there—illuminated.

I have since recovered from that initial shock, but it took a while. And as time goes on there is more to see, so it actually doesn't become an increasingly pleasant experience. It's just something you know you have to do and you are more prepared to endure it.

Seeing yourself the way *God* sees you is like looking into a giant magnifying mirror of your entire being. But He sees you from the perspective of all He made you to be. He sees all the gifts, purpose, and potential in you, having been put there by the One who not only thought about you *before* you were born but had a plan for your life.

We too often see only the negative things in ourselves. We painfully observe where we are weak, lacking, or failing. God sees all that too, but He doesn't consider it all bad.

For example, God sees your *weakness* as an opportunity for you to trust Him to be strong in you. Your weakness surrendered to God enables you to gain strength from Him beyond anything you could ever have without Him.

God sees whatever you *lack* as a possibility that you will turn to Him and declare your dependence on Him so He can supply all your needs.

God sees your *failure* as an invitation for you to walk closely with Him, so He can empower you to accomplish what you couldn't begin to do on your own.

If you are not certain about all of this, then I invite you to seek God beyond what you ever have before and come to know Him better. The better you know who God really is, the more you will recognize how much you need Him. And needing Him is always a good thing.

Understanding God's Perspective

The more we seek to know God in greater depth, the more He shows us about *Himself.* When we truly open up to God and invite Him to reveal Himself to us, He will do that. And this is something we must do. For we will never know who *we* really are until we understand who *He* really is.

God also shows us the truth about ourselves when we ask Him to do so. That can seem daunting, but don't let the idea scare you.

The good news is that He doesn't let us see everything at once—both about *Him* and about *ourselves*—which would be overwhelming in either case. He lets us see a little at a time as we seek Him.

If you have a heart that longs to know the truth and yearns for a way to become all you were created to be, spend time with God every day getting to know Him. Truly understanding His amazing goodness, holiness, perfection, and love is healing for your soul. It also exposes any lack of goodness, holiness, perfection, and love in you. But don't be afraid of that. He doesn't expose these things to shock or demean you. He does it to let you know that He loves you enough to not leave you the way you are. He wants you to become all He created you to be even more than *you* do, because His desire is for you to live in a way that opens you to the countless blessings He has for you.

From God's perspective, He sees all you will be missing if you don't seek His presence and His will in your life.

Even when we think we have walked with the Lord long enough to have taken care of most of our imperfections, we find there is always more work to be done on a deeper level. That's why we can never assume we are beyond our weakest tendencies. Or that we can make it through a day without total dependence on God and His Spirit in us enabling us to be the person He created us to be.

God wants us to become more *like* Him every day.

Notice I did *not* say we *become* God. I said we become more *like* God.

The truth is, we all need to be changed. God said we are made in His *image*, but He wants us to become *partakers of His "divine nature"* (2 Peter 1:4). That means *opening our heart to God* and *allowing Him to mold and expand it so that we can contain more of His character.*

How does that happen?

That question will be answered as you read this book. For now, just know that God wants you to become more like Him. He wants you to not only see what needs to be changed, but also to see yourself through His eyes of love.

God is lovingly forgiving, something a magnifying mirror is not.

With all that said, a few years back I was reading through the Bible from Genesis to Revelation—as is my habit to do every couple of years—and on one particular day I was starting at 1 Corinthians 13. I had read that passage countless times before and knew it was the chapter on love. In fact, it was so familiar to me that I had many of the verses memorized just from reading them over and over. And anyone who is married will find themselves reading that chapter again and again, praying that their spouse will somehow really get it. (I'm only kidding. I have learned to pray that *I* really get it. I just wanted to see your reaction.)

You know how you can read a passage of Scripture many times and each time your understanding of it deepens? It becomes increasingly etched upon your mind, soul, and spirit. But then one day— as you are again reading that same passage, about which you have asked God to give you greater understanding—it's as if the heavens opened and you have clarity about it beyond what you have ever had before. You see with such sharpness of mind, soul, and spirit that you know it is only made possible by revelation from God. Well, that is what happened to me on that day.

I had walked with the Lord for decades and thought I understood a great deal about God's love for us. And I knew how to express my love for Him, even though I realized it was an ongoing growth process. I believed I was a loving person because God had given me a deep love for other people, something I never thought possible before I began walking with Him. But on that morning— after I asked God to teach me things I had not yet seen before in this chapter, the way I always do before I read His Word—it was as though my eyes were seeing these verses in great depth and clarity for the first time. The Holy Spirit did what I asked and gave me a profound understanding of each sentence and word, as if Jesus Himself spoke them to me.

Like a giant curtain opening in heaven, I could see what was behind it and a whole new world opened up to me. It was similar to an out-of-focus picture—that I did not realize was out of focus—suddenly coming into view with crystal clarity, and I could see things I had not seen before. It was mesmerizing. It was breathtaking. It was convicting and humbling. I was gripped by every word. It was as if I had been in a dimly lit room when the roof suddenly opened up and the sun poured in, bringing eye-squinting illumination.

Each word was instantly magnified to reveal all aspects of its meaning. And with every revelation I was deeply repentant. Every description brought to mind how many times I had fallen short of choosing to show love in that specific way to someone else. It was not that I was unloving to them. It's that *my* love fell far short of what God wanted from me. Even though I knew I had come a great distance from where I had been, I was still so far from where God wanted me to be. I realized that the way God required me to show love to others was not something I could begin to do on my own. I needed the transformative power of *His* love working in me and enabling me. That meant I had to daily come to Him in order to not only be freshly infused with His love for me, but also to express my love for Him and then ask Him to help me show His love to others. I had previously thought of love as more a feeling than a choice. But these were clear choices I had to make.

Different levels of truth are in God's Word, and we must be ready to see them as God enables us.

The first number of times I read this love passage, I understood it to be the ideal. That is, the goal we should *work toward*. And it is. But that's not all.

The next level of understanding I had with regard to this passage was that God is love, and we must endeavor to be more like

Him and learn to love the way *He* does. This is also true. But there is still more.

The latest level of understanding God revealed to me was that we cannot possibly love others the way He does without His love flowing through us and enabling us. That means we must not only have an ever-deepening understanding of God's love for us, but *we must also choose to receive the love God has for us in all its fullness.*

That morning as I continued to read and reread those verses describing what love is from *God's* perspective, He brought to my mind in clear detail how I had not lived up to this standard in any one of them. I knew it wasn't out of judgment that He revealed all of this. I did not feel condemnation. I felt His *conviction.*

I felt His *love.*

It was God saying to my heart, "I want you to move on in your life and receive everything I have for you, but there are certain choices you need to make."

It was me saying, "Oh, I see now." And not, "How could I have been so stupid and blind?"

God revealed to me that I was shutting off certain blessings from my life because I didn't recognize the areas of opportunity He had placed in front of me to not only *receive His love and show my love to Him, but to also choose to love others in a way that pleased Him.* I recognized how *not choosing* to show love in certain situations in my past had worked to my detriment. I had forfeited many blessings by not making better choices.

God showed all of this to me in just moments. He taught me that when I am hesitant to deliberately show love in a certain situation, I should ask Him to reveal to me—through His Spirit speaking to my heart—what the loving thing is to do at that time. He spoke to my heart that choices are to be made, and it's not always so clear without *His* revelation what that means in that moment. What we might *think* in the flesh is the loving thing to do could actually be the *wrong* thing. That's why it's extremely important to not only have solid knowledge of God's Word, but also have the wisdom of God—especially when it requires a choice that affects other people's lives. Does my choosing to do what *I* think is the loving thing for this person actually hurt them? That can happen.

All this struck me so deeply that I nearly fell off the couch on my face before God in sorrow and repentance. This became one of those life-changing moments with God you never forget and from which you never step back. Everything—or just about everything—in this book is what God showed me in those moments.

As I continued to contemplate what happened, it became increasingly clear that none of us can begin to show love the way God wants us to without first making these choices.

Three Simple Choices That Will Alter the Course of Your Life

Our first choice is to not only understand God's love for us, but to actually open up and receive it. Yes, receiving God's love is a choice. We can *read* about it, *talk* about it, and *think* about it, but it's not the same as *choosing* to receive it. Choosing to receive God's love means getting close to Him, spending time in His presence, opening your heart to Him, seeking to know Him, understanding who He is, and desiring to become more *like* Him.

Choosing to receive God's love changes your life.

Our second choice is to deliberately choose to express our love for God in response to His love for us. We must understand how to communicate our love for Him beyond just "feeling" it. We can't do nothing in response. And we really can't love others in a powerful way without first learning to show our love for God. That's because it's the actual process of showing our love for God that becomes the very means by which He fills us with *more* of His love. The truth is, God imparts His love to us when we demonstrate our love for Him. (More about that in chapter 10.)

Choosing to express your love for God transforms your life.

Our third choice is to love others in a way that pleases God. That means we must seek God to understand what pleases Him and choose to do it instead of waiting for feelings to motivate us. Human love fails. We are incapable of loving consistently—all the time, in all the ways God wants us to—the way *He* does. Truly loving others happens when we choose to love God and He pours Himself into us.

Choosing to show love to others alters the course of your life.

These three choices make up the three sections of this book. In order to choose love the way God wants us to, we must make these three decisions every day.

The Way God Sees You

We don't naturally see ourselves the way God sees us. We see ourselves through our past. Our failures. Our work. Our abilities. Our appearance. Our friends. Our accomplishments. Or lack thereof.

We see ourselves through the prism of our flaws.

He sees us through the light of His perfection shining in our hearts, perfecting us until we go to be with Him.

We know what we are *made of,* and we don't always view that as a good thing.

He sees us in light of all *He* lovingly *made us to be.* And that is always a great thing.

I want you to see yourself the way God sees you. God sees you through His perspective of love. I want you to see yourself from God's perspective so you can better understand the love He has for you—and the far-reaching effect His love has on your life when you choose to fully open up to it.

When you receive God's love for you, it will ignite your heart, jump-start your entire being, and energize you—mind, soul, and body.

I want you to not only know God better, but to *experience* God. God is not just loving; He *is* love. And when you experience His

love *in* you, it will change your life and affect everyone with whom
you come in contact. When you choose to show God's love to others, it will not only dramatically affect *their* lives, but it will also alter
the course of *yours*.

When seeing your life through God's eyes of love, the good
will be magnified and illuminated. The bad will not be so ominous because God's love will crowd it out. Every day you choose to
receive God's love, *express* your love to Him, and *love others* the way
He wants you to, you will know He is working in you a pathway to
becoming more like Him.

There is no greater force in the world than God's love. All the
weapons of hate and cruelty cannot stand against it. The spiritually
blind and intentionally evil try to oppose it, but they cannot ultimately win. That's because all creation was formed and is sustained
by God. And He gives each of us a free will to choose His love for
our lives—or not.

Prayer of *Love*

LORD, help me to see myself the way You see me. Thank You that You see me through Your eyes of love and all You created me to be. Enable me to open up my heart to receive Your love. Although it's hard to comprehend a love so great, and I don't feel worthy of it, I don't want to shut myself off from the power of Your amazing love working in my heart. Teach me about the ways You love me that I'm not understanding. Give me eyes to see how You reveal Your love for me by keeping me from things that are not Your greatest good for my life. I know that everything You want to do in my life cannot be accomplished without Your love flowing in me.

Help me turn my gaze from myself to You. I want to see You more clearly and understand You more fully. Thank You that You not only love me, but You will enable me to understand the depth of Your love. Show me the ways I don't recognize or open up to Your love—whether because of serious doubt or simply a lack of understanding—and I have missed many of Your blessings because of it.

Enable me to see my life from Your perspective. Instead of looking through a magnifying lens to see the flaws in myself, help me to see through the magnifying lens of Your loving heart to observe the good—and potential for greatness—you have put in me. May Your presence be magnified in my life beyond what I can even imagine now. Cause Your perfection, beauty, love, and holiness to be reflected in me at all times.

In Jesus' name I pray.

Words of *Love*

How precious also are Your thoughts to me, O God!
How great is the sum of them!
If I should count them, they would be
more in number than the sand;
when I awake, I am still with You.

PSALM 139:17-18

LORD, what is man, that You take knowledge of him?
Or the son of man, that You are mindful of him?
Man is like a breath; His days are like a passing shadow.

PSALM 144:3-4

Does He not see my ways, and count all my steps?

JOB 31:4

His divine power has given to us all things that pertain to
life and godliness…by which have been given to us
exceedingly great and precious promises,
that through these you may be partakers of
the divine nature,
having escaped the corruption
that is in the world through lust.

2 PETER 1:3-4

2

Understand Who
God Really Is

~~~~~~

Nothing is more important in our lives than love. We all *need* it. We all *want it.* We *cannot live without it.* We *demand it* of others. We do desperate and crazy things for it. We reject those who won't extend it. When we are rejected by the object of our love, that touches a deep, dark, empty, dangerous place within us. Without love we can sink to the lowest pit of depression, anger, bitterness, self-hatred, and hopelessness.

Those who don't think they need love in a desperate way haven't really known life without it.

The *L* word is the obsession of every songwriter and poet, every romantic letter writer and novelist, every young and idealistic heart, and every abandoned or rejected boy or girl, man or woman.

The need for love is not restricted by gender, age, level of mental or physical health, financial circumstances, or education. We don't age out of our need for love; we just learn as we go along how to cover it better. We don't educate ourselves out of our need for love; we just learn to express it in a way that is less frightening to others. And we may have the best friends money can buy and be talked into thinking their love is the real deal, but if their love runs out when the money runs out, then we weren't the true object of their love after all.

Sometimes people may love us but don't show it in a perceivable way, so we don't feel it and therefore don't believe we're loved at all. And when we *feel* we are unloved, we may be able to cover up the inner devastation of unmet needs, but we still suffer silently. We may actually be loved, but because we don't believe we are, then being unloved is our reality.

The problem with human love is that it's fragile and weak and fraught with failure. Human love is limited. It's changeable. It can be selfishly motivated and manipulating. It's conditional and undependable. Yet we wither and die without it. Some people will take anything—no matter how meager the emotional crumbs are that fall under the table of what resembles some kind of love—rather than have nothing. We are all ecstatic when we feel love and miserable when we don't.

Many of us suffer because we think that if people don't really love us, then we will have to live forever without love. But it's not true. The greatest sense of love, which is available for us at all times, is God's love. His love is not like human love. God's love is unchanging and unfailing. That's because *He* is unchanging and unfailing. His love is unconditional. Too many of us don't understand the feast of His love waiting for us in the banquet hall of His favor.

I'm not saying we don't need human love. We certainly do, but human love has limits. God's love does not. If we think we can put all our hopes in human love, we are setting ourselves up for deep disappointment. Only God's love is fully healing, restoring, rejuvenating, and life-giving. Human love can only provide a small fraction of that, and only for so long before it becomes selfish again.

Only God's love strengthens and fortifies us like nothing else can. Only God's love can totally fill the need to be loved. Only God's love *in* us can cause us to love others without fail. We cannot live without God's love, but often people don't know it's *His* love they need. And that's because they don't know *Him*. Even if they believe He exists but have not opened up to *receive* all He *has* for them, they don't begin to comprehend the depth of His love for them.

The truth is, God loves you more than any human ever could—beyond what you can even fathom. And if you have felt unloved in your past—if love was withheld from you in your childhood or if you have been rejected in some way—you will have a harder time receiving love from God. That's because you have learned to not trust love, no matter who the source is. In order to know the depth of God's *love*, you need to know *God*.

And that's the problem.

Many people don't really know God, so they don't know His love. They know what good, bad, or erroneous things people have told them *about* God, but they don't know *Him*. And I am talking about some of the many who believe in Him as well as those who doubt Him. Understanding God's love for us is a never-ending quest that will not be fully realized until we are with Him in heaven.

In order to know God and receive His love, we need to understand who He is and how great His love is for us. We need to comprehend it at least somewhat before we can feel it. What some may believe is God's judgment on them could actually be His love shown in ways they don't yet understand. Many of us don't realize how He protects us from dangers we don't even recognize are there. As your knowledge of God grows, so will your faith in Him. As your understanding of God's nature expands, so will your love for Him.

Knowing God's eternal nature is important because the depth of your faith in Him is reflected in the size of God in your heart and your understanding.

Some Things You Must Know About God

In order to understand God's love, you need to understand who He is. Sometimes we think we know who God is, but if we ever doubt His love for us, then we don't really know Him. What follows are some basic things you need to know about God.

God was not created. He has always been. He has always existed and will always exist (Psalm 90:1-2). That means everything about

Him is forever. It's eternal. That means His love for you is forever
and will always exist.

God is the all-knowing Creator of all things. That means He knows
everything about you. He knew the moment of your conception,
and He had a plan and purpose for your life from the beginning.
God did not necessarily determine the circumstances of your conception. That was decided by the free will of at least one of your
birth parents. But if those circumstances were less than desirable,
that doesn't make you a mistake or less than desirable. You may
have been a surprise to your parents, but you were never a surprise
to God. You were born with God's plan for your salvation, restoration, redemption, and future already in place. That doesn't mean it
was all predestined. It still requires a choice from you. He has been
drawing you to Himself since you were born, but you still have to
receive Him. No matter what has happened in your past, God has
been extending His hand to you, waiting for you to open your heart
to Him.

God can touch and transform anyone with His love. No one is so
far gone that God cannot redeem and bring to triumph that person when the heart is open to receive His love. There is no pit we
can sink into that God does not reach in and pull us out of when
we look up to Him. And when we submit our own will to His and
seek His presence and help, He opens our spiritual eyes to see more
of who He really is.

You must also know that God is one God. But there are three distinct, eternal, coexistent persons in the Godhead.

There is God the Father, who was not created but has always
been.

There is Jesus, who is God's Son and also God. He, too, was not
created but was begotten by His Father God.

There is also the Holy Spirit, who *proceeds from* God and is God's
Spirit and also God.

In the beginning the Father, Son, and Holy Spirit were together at creation. And when they created man, God said, "Let *Us* make man in *Our* image, according to *Our* likeness" (Genesis 1:26).

Who is "*Us*"?

"Us" refers to these three—Father, Son, and Holy Spirit—who are separate and distinct but are also inseparable. And they are as active in your life as you welcome them to be. In order to know God, you have to know each of these three persons of the Trinity. To leave out one is to have an incomplete picture of God—God the Father, God the Son, and God the Holy Spirit. Any lopsided view will limit all God can do in your life.

Our image of who God is shapes the way we respond to Him. For many people, their image of God comes from their experience. It is formed by what they have seen in other believers, or what they learned in church, or what the people who were most influential in their lives taught them. If they were disappointed in people who were supposed to be God's people, then they put that disappointment on God. They blame God for the abuse they received from those who were supposed to love and protect them and did not.

People also tend to view God the way they viewed their father, or father figure, in their life. If that was not a positive image for them, then they may also put that human failure on God. For example, if your father abandoned you in any way, you may feel that your heavenly Father has or will also abandon you too, and therefore you cannot trust Him. If your earthly father was never there for you, you may feel that your heavenly Father won't be there for you either. If your human father was distant, you may feel your heavenly Father is distant as well.

If you have rejected God for whatever reason, or have hesitated to open up to Him and receive His healing and restoring love, please know that He is not angry with you. He knows that it takes knowing Him and His unconditional love for you before you can gain total trust in Him. But He wants you to do that as soon as possible. That's because the sooner you open up to fully receiving His love, the sooner you can receive all He has for you—which is far more than you can imagine. Even if you have known God for years, there is always more to learn about Him.

Some people think it takes mindless faith to believe in God, but it actually takes blind and reckless faith to look at this beautiful world and amazing universe and believe there is *no* God.

King David, a man after God's own heart, said that only a fool says "there is no God." He said these kinds of people become corrupt and "there is none who does good" (Psalm 14:1). That's because if there is no God, then there are no absolutes, no moral law, and no final restriction on behavior. They can make up their own law and change it whenever they want. They are definitely not motivated by love.

David said that truly "the heavens declare the glory of God; and the firmament shows His handiwork" (Psalm 19:1). That means God is revealed and can be seen in His creation. "The heavens declare His righteousness, and all the peoples see His glory" (Psalm 97:6). A person has to be *spiritually blind by choice* in order to not see God's goodness and greatness.

The evidence for God is everywhere.

One of the ways God shows His love to us is in all that He has made—in His creation. It is here for *our* enjoyment and appreciation as well as His own pleasure. "Come and see the works of God; He is awesome in His doing toward the sons of men" (Psalm 66:5).

His works are evidence of His love for us.

Some people (theists) believe God is the Creator and the giver of life. Others (naturalists) believe there is no God and nothing exists outside of what is in the physical world. They say there is no spiritual world because they can't see it. But their spiritual eyes are not open; therefore, they cannot see spiritual things. They influence others into believing God does not exist even though they cannot prove it. They say that God is a myth, a figment of imagination. They say He is dead, not even pausing to account for the fact that if He is dead, He must have been alive, therefore He must have existed. And if He is dead, where is He buried and what happened at the funeral? They have no answers.

Some people *choose* to believe God never existed. They point to everything bad and say, "If there is a God, how could He allow all the evil in the world?" But the truth is, all the evil in the world exists because of those who *chose* to separate themselves from God and His ways. They now choose to serve evil over serving God.

God is real. Evil is also real. We have a choice between two realities. And we must make that choice as to which one we will serve.

God, the Creator of Everything, Did Not Create Evil

God is the Creator of all things, but He did not create evil. He did create beautiful angelic beings to dwell in heaven with Him. However, the most beautiful angelic being of all created by God was an archangel called "Lucifer," among other names. His name means "day star," "shining one," "light-bringer," "sun of the morning," and "light-bearer." He was the luciferous one—so beautiful that he became enthralled with his own beauty. In his self-focused, self-centered, and prideful manner, he chose his own will over God's will. He wanted to *be* God instead of *serve* God. So he rebelled against God, influencing a third of the angels to go along with him. As a result, he and they fell to earth and became Satan and his demons.

Isaiah said of Lucifer, "How you are fallen from heaven" (Isaiah 14:12).

Jesus said of Lucifer, "I saw Satan fall like lightning from heaven" (Luke 10:18). Jesus wanted to assure His disciples that He had witnessed Satan's fall and had now given them "authority…over all the power of the enemy" (Luke 10:19).

Before Lucifer/Satan fell, he made his pride and self-will known in five proclamations against God in Isaiah 14:13-14, all starting with "I will." He said:

"I will ascend into heaven."

"I will exalt my throne above the stars of God."

"I will also sit on the mount of the congregation."

"I will ascend above the heights of the clouds."

"I will be like the Most High."

He was so full of himself that his pride motivated him to make a terrible choice. As a result, he lost his position as the leader of worship in God's kingdom because he worshipped himself instead of God. But God, as always, had the final word. He countered every threat Lucifer made, saying he could no longer claim any of the beautiful names describing him and he would end up in the lowest pit of hell. Once a beautiful created being, by his own self-will he became independent from God and fell from everything God had for him. (In Isaiah 14, Isaiah is also referring to the evil king of Babylon, who acted like the devil and is foreseeing that because of the king's pride he will be brought down in the same way Satan was.) By choice, Satan became God's enemy—the opposite of God—and is the source of evil in the world.

God is not the source of evil in your world or in your life. Yet when evil manifests, many people blame God for it. But it is actually God's enemy—and yours—trying to destroy you and others. Evil does not exist because of a lack of God's love. Evil exists because of a choice to rebel against God and reject His love.

The power of evil is real, but God's power is far greater. Evil gains power through deception—that is, getting people to believe lies about God and reject God's truth. The power of evil is sustained by those who choose it and support it. When you are on God's side— when you choose to open your heart to God and receive His love— the enemy will try to influence you to believe lies about God.

Everything you don't know about God will be used against you by the enemy of your soul.

Read the sentence above 20 more times or until it is etched in your mind.

One of the reasons you need to know God well—*who* He is, *what* He does, and *all* He can and will do in your life—is that the enemy will try to deceive you about each of these things and tempt you into losing hope and faith in God. What follows are some of the things you need to know about God that the enemy, and the people who do his bidding, do not want you to know and will lie to you about them.

You Must Know God Created You

It is important to understand that you were not randomly spawned. God made you with a spirit and soul. You were not an accident.

David said, "*You formed my inward parts; You covered me in my mother's womb.* I will praise You, for *I am fearfully and wonderfully made*; marvelous are Your works, and that my soul knows very well…*Your eyes saw my substance, being yet unformed. And in Your book they all were written, the days fashioned for me, when as yet there were none of them*" (Psalm 139:13-16).

The same is true of you. God saw you as you were growing in your mother's womb. All your days are recorded in His book of your life. One or both of your parents may have failed you, but God has not and will not. He has loved you from the beginning, and He waits for you to open up to receive His love.

The enemy may come to tell you that you are an accident—unplanned, unwanted, and without purpose—and nothing good will happen to you unless you make it happen or you sell out to him to make it happen. But quite the opposite is true. Never allow the enemy of your soul to tell you any differently.

You Must Know God's Love Is Real

God's love is real because *He* is real. And He is love.

Remember, God doesn't just *have* love; He *is* love. That is who He is. And His love is there for anyone who opens up their heart to it.

Human love is like a vapor you can't see unless someone chooses to demonstrate it in what they say or do, but God's love *can be* seen. When your spiritual eyes are opened, you can see manifestations of His love all over your life. Those who don't sense God's love don't really know Him. Jesus said to some of those who did not receive Him, "I know you, that *you do not have the love of God in you*" (John 5:42). He recognized that they did not have God's love in them and therefore did not really know God. Many people don't really believe God loves them because they don't know Him.

Do you really know that God loves you? Do you truly believe it? Do you actually feel it or sense it? Because if you don't, He has so much more waiting for you to receive from Him.

If you *do* believe God loves you, is it personal? Do you ever doubt it? Do you see the manifestations of His love for you every day?

It's easy to understand why people don't recognize God's love for them when they have been through many difficult or tragic things and are bruised, wounded, damaged, and hurt. They think, *Where is God in all this? He must not be there for me.*

The truth is, God is always where He is asked to be. Yes, God is every-where. But the great manifestations of His love and power are only clearly seen wherever He is invited to be.

Too many people don't invite Him into their lives in any way and then wonder why He doesn't do their bidding. Have you invited God to manifest Himself in your life? If not, it's never too late.

If you have already invited God into your life, ask Him to reveal Himself to you in a new and deeper way. No matter how long we have walked with the Lord, we all continue to need greater revelation of Him and His love for us.

Don't let the enemy—or anyone who serves God's enemy—tell you that God and His unending love for you are not real.

You Must Know God Is Good

God is good all the time, and you can trust that—even when bad things happen. We all know bad things happen to good people, but all of us are really only good to the degree that we allow God's goodness to flow into us. We keep that from happening when we resist the flow of His goodness and love to us in some way.

That's why it is important to grow daily in our knowledge of God. We not only need to learn new things about Him—because there is always more to learn—but we must also understand new depths of the things we already know. For example, we may know that God is good, but it will be a never-ending journey of discovery as to *how* good God is. We may already know that God loves us, but we will be ever-learning that no matter how much we *think* He loves us, it is far more than we can even fathom.

I have heard too many comments from people saying something like, "I don't know if I can believe in a god who allowed this bad thing to happen," as if God exists according to the way we believe. We don't have a designer god whom we design according to what we want. That would, by mere definition, not be God. The truth is, God *is* who He is. And we cannot alter that fact no matter what we believe.

It is the height of arrogance to think *we* can decide who God is. He already *is*. What we *do* decide is whether to believe in who He is.

"God said to Moses, 'I AM WHO I AM'" (Exodus 3:14).

God is who He is, and it is up to us to decide whether to learn more about Him. We do that by spending time with Him in His Word and in prayer. The more we know *about* Him, the better we will know Him and the deeper our love for Him will grow. Just recognizing that He exists and is the God who can be known is the first step. It is not up to us to make God in our image. We are made in *His*. *God is who He is, and we do not affect or change that in any way.*

We must hold steadfastly to this truth that the psalmist said about God: "I *would have lost heart, unless I had believed that I would see the goodness of the LORD* in the land of the living" (Psalm 27:13).

Too often we lose heart when things don't go our way because we don't firmly trust God and His loving-kindness toward us. God's Word invites us to "*taste and see that the LORD is good*; blessed is the man who trusts in Him!" (Psalm 34:8).

David often instructed his own soul to do the right thing. He said, "O my soul, you have said to the Lord, '*You are my Lord, my goodness is nothing apart from You*'" (Psalm 16:2). *Apart from God's goodness poured into our lives, our goodness is limited.*

It's not enough to only remember that God is good. We must also praise Him for His goodness. The Bible says, "The earth is full of the goodness of the Lord" (Psalm 33:5). "Oh, that men would give thanks to the Lord for His goodness, and for His wonderful works to the children of men!" (Psalm 107:8).

Whatever we praise God for, the enemy cannot use against us.

God is good. Don't let anyone tell you any differently. Whoever tries to convince you that God is not good doesn't have your best interests at heart.

You Must Know God Is Holy

Holiness is one of God's main attributes. In fact, everything about Him can be seen in the light of His love and holiness.

We are made in God's image, but we do not have any of His attributes without His enablement. We can only live in holiness as we are willing to separate ourselves from all that is unholy or ungodly and look to Him to fill us with Himself.

Moses said, "Who is like You, O Lord, among the gods? *Who is like You, glorious in holiness,* fearful in praises, doing wonders?" (Exodus 15:11).

Hannah, a devoted servant of the Lord said, "*No one is holy like the Lord,* for there is none besides You, nor is there any rock like our God" (1 Samuel 2:2).

David said, "Give unto the Lord the glory due to His name; *worship the Lord in the beauty of holiness*" (Psalm 29:2).

Holiness brings wholeness. God's holiness in you makes you whole. When you open up to His love, you become a vessel into which He pours Himself. So don't fall for the lie that you can never attain the holiness described in God's Word. You can't attain it by yourself, but with God you most certainly can.

You Must Know God Is Unchanging

"Changeable" is our middle name without God's Spirit in us giving us an anchor in our heart, soul, and spirit. We are capable of changing by the minute. You know how some people can be nice one moment and raging lunatics the next? We are all changeable— perhaps not generally to that extent—no matter how solid we may appear at the moment. I've seen the most stable person I know in the Lord change into someone who acts as though he doesn't know God at all. And it happened because he thought he couldn't fail. He became influenced by people who did not know God because he did not stay strong in the things he once knew about God.

God never changes. You can depend on that. The psalmist said to God, "You are the same, and Your years will have no end" (Psalm 102:27).

God has always been and will always be.

It's hard for us to grasp the concept of always being. We cannot imagine anyone who was not created and didn't have a beginning. *We* have *not always been.* But we *will always be.* The important question is, where will we always be? And *who will* we always be *with*?

God is eternal. And we are given the choice to either spend eternity *with* Him or *apart* from Him. When we make the decision to walk *with* Him, our eternal future is secure. That does not change because *He* does not change. When you walk with God, you are always walking into the future He has for you.

You Must Know God Is All-Powerful and Nothing Is Impossible for Him

The power of God is greater than the power of the greatest hurricane, flood, tornado, earthquake, or tsunami. "*The* LORD *on high is mightier than the noise of many waters*, than the mighty waves of the sea" (Psalm 93:4). "*The mountains melt like wax at the presence of the* LORD, at the presence of the Lord of the whole earth" (Psalm 97:5).

One of the greatest things about God is that He shares Himself with you. And that means He shares His power. But you are empowered only as you give place to God's love working in your life.　　　　-

Don't let your mind be swayed into questioning that.

God is all-powerful. That means nothing is impossible for Him where you are concerned. You may be facing impossible circumstances and cannot see a way *out*, but God can. He can also see a way *through*. Don't doubt that. Don't think you have to turn to the dark side in difficult times. That is one of the biggest lies the enemy will use against you. Know where your power source is found and do not seek another. In God you have access to all the power you will ever need to live the life He has for you.

You Must Know God Owns Everything and Knows What You Need

Because God created everything, that means He owns everything, which is more than enough for what you and I need. God said, "Every beast of the forest is Mine, and *the cattle on a thousand hills*...the world is Mine, and all its fullness" (Psalm 50:10,12).

David said, "The earth is the Lord's, and all its fullness, the world and those who dwell therein" (Psalm 24:1). Everything in our world, including us, belongs to God.

God shows His love by giving the earth to us. "The heaven, even the heavens, are the Lord's; *but the earth He has given to the children of men*" (Psalm 115:16). Still, He wants us to look to Him to be our Provider.

Jesus said, "*Your Father knows the things you have need of before you ask Him*" (Matthew 6:8). God knows what you need, and He is more than able to supply everything you need, but He wants you to come to Him in prayer and ask. God is always all about a relationship with you. He is not interested in being Santa Claus or your personal sugar daddy. God hears your prayers and answers them when you pray from a pure heart that loves Him.

When we don't know Him well, or at all, we often don't understand His answers. We think that if He doesn't answer in the way we prayed, then He didn't hear. Prayer is not dictating to God and telling Him what to do. It is partnering with God in every aspect of your life.

Understand that no matter what anyone says to the contrary, God renews and replenishes the earth.

This may be a shock for the predictors of doom. If we were to live God's way instead of thinking we know better than God, we would not run out of whatever we need. When we do evil, God hides His face from us (Psalm 104:29). But when we live His way, He replenishes the earth (Psalm 104:30).

Don't let fear of not having enough cause you to doubt that God will provide. Continue to seek Him for provision for your life. He is your Provider, and He has all you need.

You Must Know God Is All-Seeing

God sees everything at all times. Nothing you think or do is hidden from Him. He sees where you are and where you're going. He also sees where you are *supposed* to be going and how to get you there. "There is nothing covered that will not be revealed, and hidden that will not be known" (Matthew 10:26). "O God, You know my foolishness; and my sins are not hidden from You" (Psalm 69:5).

God doesn't keep a record of all you do in order to embarrass you at some later date, or to hold it over your head as a threat, or to have a case against you so you can be punished. He does it because He loves you. He even sees the tears you shed. David said, "You number my wanderings; put my tears into Your bottle; are they not in Your book?" (Psalm 56:8).

God knows you better than you know yourself. He sees the enemy's plans for your destruction, and when He hears your prayers He sees His answers to them long before you do. Don't think that God does not see your pain, struggle, fear, and circumstances. His eye is on you and He watches over you. He is with you as long as you are with Him.

Prayer of *Love*

LORD, I long to know You better. Teach me all about You. I know I cannot begin to comprehend Your greatness without Your opening my eyes, enlarging my heart and mind, and giving me revelation. "O LORD my God, You are very great: You are clothed with honor and majesty, who cover Yourself with light as with a garment, who stretch out the heavens like a curtain" (Psalm 104:1-2). Help me to understand all that You are so that I can grow ever deeper in my walk with You.

Enable me to comprehend all that You do. Help me to remember at all times that You never change. You are who You are, and no lies of the enemy can alter that in any way. "Your throne is established from of old; You are from everlasting" (Psalm 93:2). "You, LORD, are most high above all the earth; You are exalted far above all gods" (Psalm 97:9). I pray that the essence and character of who You are will transform me and guide who I become.

I cannot fathom Your *love* for me without understanding all You have *done* for me. Enable me to fully open my heart and mind to receive that wonderful knowledge of You. Thank You that Your love is unconditional, unchanging, and unfailing. Teach me to understand and acknowledge all the ways You demonstrate Your love toward me. Fortify my spirit so I never doubt it. Help me trust at all times that Your love is real and true and always there for me in unlimited supply. Thank You that Your loving-kindness and goodness toward me never fail.

In Jesus' name I pray.

Words of *Love*

Lord, You have been our dwelling place in all generations.
Before the mountains were brought forth,
or ever You had formed the earth
and the world, even from everlasting to everlasting, You
are God.

PSALM 90:1-2

A thousand years in Your sight are like yesterday
when it is past,
and like a watch in the night.

PSALM 90:4

He lays the beams of His upper chambers in the waters,
who makes the clouds His chariot,
who walks on the wings of the wind,
who makes His angels spirits, His ministers a flame of fire.

PSALM 104:3-4

Judge nothing before the time, until the Lord comes,
who will both bring to light the hidden things of darkness
and reveal the counsels of the hearts.
Then each one's praise will come from God.

1 CORINTHIANS 4:5

3

Receive All
God Has for You

~~~~~~

God's love for us existed long before *we* existed. That means He certainly loved us way before we even thought about loving Him. "I have loved you with an *everlasting love*," He said. "Therefore with lovingkindness I have *drawn you*" (Jeremiah 31:3).

That's the way He *is*.

This means on all those days when we weren't thinking about *Him*—and we were living our own way and not living for *Him*—He was still extending His hand of unfailing love to us, reaching to draw us close to Him.

That's what He *does*.

Every day of our lives He extends His love to us. We are the ones who don't recognize it. Don't respond. Don't believe. It is we who—knowingly or not—turn away and don't receive the love He has with our name on it. Yet our *recognition* of God's unending love for us—and our *receiving* it into our heart—is what radically changes our lives. It's what makes us whole and frees us to be all we were created to be.

It's what causes our life to finally make sense.

For without God's love we are lost. We are hopeless. We are

ruined. But the day it clearly dawns on us how much He truly loves us, we never see life the same again. Now we see it from the perspective of His love and not His judgment.

That is a great day!

But how do we actually *receive* God's love, beyond simply recognizing that He loves us?

God has made a specific way.

God did not make us robots. He made thinking, decision-making people capable of choosing good over evil, truth over lies, and His ways over our own. However, He knows what we are made of. He knows that because we have freedom of choice, we can be enticed to *choose* a path *separate from Him*. That's why He had a plan to bridge that gap of separation.

He gave us a way back. A way to start over. A chance to begin again.

He gave us His greatest gift of all—His Son.

Many people have already received this gift. But He is the gift who keeps on giving. No matter how long we have known Him, we still need to keep understanding and receiving all that He has paid an unthinkable price to give us.

God chose a pure and humble young woman of faith—a virgin named Mary—to conceive a child by the power of His Holy Spirit and give birth to God's Son. She had to be a woman who walked with God and knew the Scriptures well enough to understand what was happening. She had to be the kind of person who would not run from God's call on her life. She had to have the strength and sensitivity of character to respond to God by saying, "Let it be to me according to Your word" (Luke 1:38). And she was all that.

The angel who appeared to Mary with the stunning news told her that His name was to be called *Jesus*, which means "salvation" (Luke 1:31). He would also be called *Immanuel*, meaning "*God with us*" (Matthew 1:23).

When He was born, His identity was revealed to some who had been anticipating His birth and knew why He came.

Jesus came to save us from the consequence of our mistakes, errors, bad choices, sins, and failures, which is death. He came to save us from our enemy, who tries incessantly to destroy us. He came to save us from hopelessness and futility, which we are all heir to without Him. He came to save us from ourselves.

Jesus came to sacrifice Himself and lay down His life for us so we could be with Him forever. All because He loves us.

Jesus came so that we could have good news every day of our lives.

Receiving the Love of God Through Jesus Changed My Life

When I received the Lord decades ago, I had a dramatic encounter with God. It was a life-transforming experience. One of the most amazing aspects about that time was not only sensing the love of God in the people who led me to the Lord, but also sensing God's love for *me*.

I was twenty-eight years old and felt that my life was over. I had been raised by a very abusive, mentally ill mother and locked in a closet much of my early childhood. I grew up with paralyzing fear, anxiety, depression, and hopelessness. I tried everything I could to stop the pain and find a reason to live. I went into occult practices, Eastern religions, alcohol, drugs—but nothing provided more than temporary relief, after which I was always worse than before I started down that path. Nothing worked.

My hopelessness grew to such a state that I was days away from collecting enough sleeping pills to make sure I never woke up to that unending pain again. Back in those days, sleeping pills were not so easy to come by. You had to know somebody and I didn't. But in the midst of my desperation, a friend and her pastor cared enough about me to recognize my suffering, and they met with me at a popular eating spot close to where I lived. The pastor explained God's love for me and how I could receive it. He told me about Jesus in a way that someone talks about a best friend. He said God had a plan and high purpose for my life, and He could change me from the inside out.

I had never dreamed of such a thing.

"How is that possible?" I asked.

The pastor gave me three books to read that he said would answer many of my questions. One was on the reality of evil, and God knew I needed this book because my occult practices had taught me that evil existed only in our mind. So if we got rid of evil in our mind, then it would not exist. I didn't really fall for that lie because even if you could get rid of evil in your own mind, what can you do about the evil in someone else's mind who wants to inflict it on you?

There were many of these kinds of details in the occult practices and other religions I had experimented with that didn't make sense, didn't work, and didn't produce any tangible benefit in my life. They were all about trying to work my way to God, to be acceptable to Him. But with each new endeavor that failed, I sank lower and lower until I believed there was no other way to rid myself of emotional pain other than to end my life.

The second book I was given that day was on the work and power of the Holy Spirit in our lives when we receive Jesus. The third book was the Gospel of John. I went home and read all three books, and with each one my eyes were opened to things I had never heard before.

My friend and I went back to meet with her pastor the following week, as he had requested we do.

"Did you read the books?" he asked me right away.

"Yes, I did."

"What did you think of them?"

"I thought I was reading the truth."

He then asked if I wanted to receive Jesus. In a split-second look at my life I saw I had nothing to lose. I had tried everything I knew to do and there was no relief. No answers. I could not live with the emotional pain I was carrying around inside me another day.

I planned to end my pain one way or another. If what I felt while reading those books and hearing the pastor say was true, then this could be the best thing that ever happened to me.

I said yes.

I received the Lord that day and I felt different. I had a strange sensation in my heart that I didn't recall ever experiencing before. It was hope. For the first time in my life I felt I actually had a future.

From that time on I wanted to know everything about Jesus. I wanted to be close to Him and experience the greatness of His love for me.

Jesus Is Called the Word, the Door, and the Good Shepherd

I learned that *Jesus is called the Word.* He wasn't an afterthought by God in His creation of all things. Jesus was there *with* God and His Holy Spirit from the *beginning* of creation. The Bible says, *"In the beginning was the Word, and the Word was with God…All things were made through Him,* and without Him nothing was made that was made" (John 1:1,3). Jesus is the *living Word.* He came to earth as a man to dwell *with* us and meet us at our greatest need.

Jesus told people He was *with God* and had been *sent by God* (John 7:28-29). He said no one had seen God except for Him (John 6:46). Jesus was the only one who was sent to earth from God. *Jesus was fully God and fully man, sent as a gift of God's love for us.*

Jesus is called the door. That's because He is the only door through which we enter God's kingdom on earth and in eternity. He said, *"I am the door. If anyone enters by Me, he will be saved,* and will go in and out and find pasture" (John 10:9).

Jesus is the open door to everything we need in our lives.

We must keep that in mind at all times. *When it seems all doors are closed to us, we have forgotten who He is.*

Jesus is called the good shepherd. Referring to Himself, He said, "I am *the good shepherd;* and *I know My sheep…* and *I lay down My life for the sheep*" (John 10:14-15). He said His sheep follow Him because "they know his voice" (John 10:4). *When we receive the gift of Jesus, our spirit is awakened and we can hear His voice speaking to our heart.*

Jesus told others He was going to lay down His life for the sheep. He came to earth with the full intention of laying down His life for you and me.

There is no greater love than that.

Even though Jesus was speaking to the Jews at the time because He was born among them, He was also speaking of "other sheep" which were "not of this fold," saying they "will hear My voice; and *there will be one flock and one shepherd*" (John 10:16).

This means *people of all races are His.* And no one can take away the fact that every one of them who chooses to follow Him as their Savior and Shepherd will not only walk with Him every day of their lives but also into eternity to be with Him forever.

Jesus Is Called the Way, the Truth, and the Life

Jesus is the only way to get to where we need to go.

In fact, we cannot get there from here without Him.

I know I would never be where I am today if I had not chosen His way over my own. I am sure I would have died years ago when I had collected enough sleeping pills to end the pain.

Jesus said, "*I am the way, the truth, and the life. No one comes to the Father except through Me*" (John 14:6). He was very clear about that. Only through Jesus can we get to a place of being eternally restored into a close relationship with God and find the great peace, rest, hope, and love His presence brings us.

While God continuously sees all the good He puts in us, He also sees all our mistakes and errors, our foolishness, rebellion, and idol worship. He sees our rejection of Him and His ways and laws. Even so, it doesn't matter what we *have* or *have not* done, He still loves us enough to continue drawing us to Himself. And He gives us *free will to choose* to receive *His way* for our lives or not.

God's way is through Jesus.

Jesus gave us a way to be free of the consequences of living apart from God—which is death—and to begin again in a close relationship with God forever.

There is not a person who doesn't need to be free from the consequences of sin. This is no small matter.

Living against God's ways works death in our lives in some manner every day when we allow it to continue. But Jesus gave us a *way* to be *born anew*. The first time we were born, it was in the *flesh*, but being born *again* refers to being born in the *spirit* (John 3:6).

These are two separate events. You had no choice about the first one. You *do* have a choice about the second.

When you receive Jesus, your spirit comes alive. You experience life in a dynamic new way. You see things differently.

Jesus said, "Unless one is born again, he cannot see the kingdom of God" (John 3:3). Without Him, there is so much we cannot see that exists in the spirit realm. Good things. Amazing things. The kingdom of God is a realm of blessing we cannot penetrate unless we have been born in the spirit by choosing to receive Jesus as Lord.

Even if you received the Lord years ago, don't think you have nothing more to learn about Him. Yes, we are saved instantly from spiritual death, but His salvation takes a lifetime of working in us an ever-increasing understanding of all Jesus did.

We tend to forget the extent of what Jesus accomplished because of His love for us.

Jesus was crucified—brutally tortured and nailed to a cross until He was dead. Then He was placed in a cave-like tomb with an enormous stone rolled in front of it and guards to keep anyone from stealing His body. But three days later the stone was supernaturally rolled away and Jesus was no longer in the tomb. He had risen from the dead to prove He was who He said He was, and that He had accomplished all He said He came to do.

His resurrection was real.

More than 500 people witnessed Him in His resurrected body as He appeared to each one of them over the following days before He ascended into heaven to be with His Father God.

After Jesus had risen, He entered a securely locked room and appeared to the people inside the room. He did not need to have someone unlock and open the door for Him because He *is* the door. And He is the way through. He is the God of truth because His Spirit leads us into all truth. Those of us who know Him understand that He is alive and He is the way to life forever with Him.

Jesus Is Called Savior, Redeemer, and Restorer

Jesus is called Savior because He saved us from the consequences of our own sin, which is death. He was sinless, yet He took the consequences of *our* sin on *Himself*. And He gave us His sinlessness in exchange (2 Corinthians 5:2). That is certainly nowhere near being a fair trade for Him, but He saw His sacrifice as the right thing to do, because when you love someone you do everything in your power to save them from destruction.

Jesus is called Redeemer because He "gave Himself for us, that He might redeem us from every lawless deed and purify for Himself His own special people" (Titus 2:14). He redeemed us from our place of being lost and took us to a place of being His special people. He is continuously preparing us for the good things He has for us to do and be.

Jesus is called the Restorer because once we receive Him, God then sees the righteousness, goodness, and purity of Jesus in us. And as a result we have the right to be called children of God. As a child of God we are completely restored to Him. There is no more separation between us. "As many as received Him, to them *He gave the right to become children of God, to those who believe in His name*" (John 1:12).

What kind of love is this that we are called God's children? (1 John 3:1).

Being a child of God makes us joint heirs with Jesus. That means everything Jesus is heir to, we also inherit. Except, of course, the right to sit at God's right hand in heaven. Only Jesus has paid the price for that honor.

Jesus *willingly* laid down His life. Because He is God, He could have stepped down from the cross at any time and said, "Forget this. I am not doing it. These people are not worth it."

Instead, even though He would have liked to not endure what was ahead, He prayed to God saying, "Not My will, but Yours, be done" (Luke 22:42).

Love kept Jesus going to the cross—love for His Father God and love for us.

What follows in this chapter are only *some* of the gifts Jesus died to give us. When I truly understood these things, they changed my life.

When You Receive Jesus, He Gives You a New Foundation

Think about receiving a gift. Let's say a valuable cross in a frame. I was given such a gift one time. If I had never opened up the gift, would I have really received the cross? If after years had passed, and it was still sitting inside the box all wrapped up in pretty paper and a bow, did I really receive it? I received something, but it was not near what was actually given.

God gives us the gift of Jesus, but too often we don't really open the gift to see what all we have been given. One of the things He gives us is an entirely new foundation upon which to build our lives.

Once you receive Jesus, *He* becomes your new foundation. The Bible says, "No other foundation can anyone lay than that which is laid, which is Jesus Christ" (1 Corinthians 3:11). Every day you walk with Him, you build on that foundation.

The great thing about a gift is that you can open it at any time. And you can start building on that foundation whenever you do.

When You Receive Jesus, You Receive Forgiveness for All of Your Wrong Choices

Our nature is nothing like God's.

All of us are born with a sinful nature (Ephesians 2:3). Left to our own ways, "there is *none who seeks after God...there is none who does good*, no, not one...*the way of peace they have not known. There is no fear of God before their eyes*" (Romans 3:11-12,17-18).

That's the way we are.

However, once we accept Jesus, we receive complete forgiveness for all our past failures to live God's way. From then on when we violate God's rules, laws, and ways, we must simply come to Him with a repentant heart and confess it. And He forgives us every time. That truth does not encourage us to keep on sinning, because we know that as long as we are unrepentant it will always be a hindrance to our lives and keep us from all God has for us.

The longer we walk in right relationship with God, "the way *we* are" becomes more like "the way *He* is."

No matter how good we think we are, every human is unrighteous in the sight of God. If we don't know how bad *sin* is, it's because we don't understand how holy *God* is. And because His holiness and our sinfulness cannot be reconciled, we will spend eternity separated from Him. The only way we can live for eternity with God is to receive Jesus and have a spiritual rebirth. It is not something we can accomplish on our own. Jesus accomplished it with His death and resurrection. *He* did it. All we do is open up to receive Him.

If we don't receive Him and are not born again in the spirit, we don't have a relationship with God and cannot experience His kingdom and the fullness of His love in our life or in the life to come. If we do not have a relationship with God, it is by our own choice.

When You Receive Jesus, God Shares Himself with You

God is everywhere, but His presence and power are only revealed and seen by those who believe in Him and choose to have a close relationship with Him on His terms. When we do that, He shares Himself with us.

One of the greatest signs of God's love for us is that when we receive Jesus, He gives us His Holy Spirit to live in us and be with us forever. In this way God shares another part of Himself—the very essence of who He is—with us.

Jesus promised that after He ascended into heaven to be with His Father God, He would send "the Helper, the Holy Spirit, whom the Father will send in My name" (John 14:26). The Holy Spirit was sent to dwell in all who received Jesus as their Lord and Savior. *The Holy Spirit is also referred to as the Spirit of Christ because God the Father, Jesus the Son, and the Holy Spirit are one.*

The Holy Spirit in us is the sign that we are *His*. The Bible says, "You are not in the flesh but in the Spirit, if indeed the Spirit of God dwells in you. *Now if anyone does not have the Spirit of Christ, he is not His*" (Romans 8:9).

The Holy Spirit is the seal that says we are the Lord's. It is a done deal and nothing can change that.

One of the greatest tragedies is that many people know even less about the Holy Spirit than they do about God and Jesus. But *God, Jesus, and the Holy Spirit are one and inseparable.* People try to divide them up and leave one or more persons of the Trinity out, but God cannot be divided into parts. If we do not recognize His Spirit in us, then we cannot receive all God has for us.

Jesus died the death we should have died because He loves us. But He didn't stop there. Now He is *with* us through the Holy Spirit who lives *in* us. We have been made righteous by receiving Jesus, and God sees the righteousness of Jesus when He looks at us. The Holy Spirit cannot dwell in an unsanctified body, but when we receive Jesus we become a sanctified temple for the Holy Spirit. Now God sends His Spirit to live in us. I'm not talking about spiritual gifts or manifestations or specific outpourings of the Holy Spirit. I'm talking simply about receiving Jesus and Him giving you His Holy Spirit to live in you.

Too many people won't even mention the Holy Spirit as if He doesn't exist or doesn't matter, but He is our eternal connection with God. "No one knows the things of God except the Spirit of God. Now *we have received, not the spirit of the world, but the Spirit who is from God,* that we might know the things that have been freely given to us by God" (1 Corinthians 2:11-12).

We receive His Spirit so we can really know Him.

God shows His love for you by giving you His presence—His Holy Spirit, part of Himself—to live in you. What a precious gift of love.

When You Receive Jesus, You Receive Everything God Has for You

When *we* give Jesus everything we have, He gives us everything *He* has. But He requires that we seek Him for all we need.

As a child of God, that means you are part of the family business. As such you receive the power of Jesus' name. Jesus said, "He who believes in Me, the works that I do he will do also; and greater works than these he will do, because I go to My Father. And *whatever you ask in My name, that I will do,* that the Father may be glorified in the Son. *If you ask anything in My name, I will do it*" (John 14:12-14).

This means everything you need can be secured by praying in Jesus' name.

We all can see how powerful the name of Jesus is when godless people don't even want His name to be spoken unless it is said as a curse word. That's not true of any other name. Why is Jesus the only name used as a curse word? It is because the realm of darkness fully recognizes the light of the Lord and tries to snuff it out. Evil works to tear down and destroy those who have the light of the Lord in them. It is proof that those who know the truth and reject it are aligned with evil. Our spiritual enemy knows exactly who Jesus is. "You believe that there is one God. You do well. Even the demons believe—and tremble!" (James 2:19).

People who misuse His name will never know the power to accomplish great things when they pray. It is a serious offense to speak His name without the reverence due Him. Those who do will sadly never know all God has for them.

When You Receive Jesus, He Gives You Victory over the Enemy

Jesus came to deliver us from the dark realm of our spiritual enemy. God *"has delivered us from the power of darkness and conveyed us into the kingdom of the Son of His love"* (Colossians 1:13). Contrasting Himself with the enemy, Jesus said, "The thief does not come except to steal, and to kill, and to destroy. *I have come that they may have life, and that they may have it more abundantly"* (John 10:10).

A big part of the abundant life Jesus came to give us includes our authority in spiritual warfare that is established on the foundation of Jesus' death on the cross. In laying down *His* life, He won victory over death and hell for *us*. Now He has given us power over the enemy when we pray in His name.

Jesus said He did not come to judge or condemn people, but rather to save and free them. Jesus freed us from whatever enslaves us. He said, "Whoever commits sin is a slave of sin" (John 8:34). And we cannot dwell in God's house as a slave of sin.

Jesus said, *"If the Son makes you free, you shall be free indeed"* (John 8:36). This means His freedom is final. His freedom has been entirely secured for us. With His death and resurrection, we don't ever have to be enslaved again.

During the first couple of years after I received Jesus, I was set free from anxiety, depression, fear, and sadness. It happened as I fasted and prayed and believers prayed for me. This freedom is what God has for all of us. Because Jesus broke the power of the enemy, I didn't have to be enslaved by darkness again.

We never have to walk in darkness. Even when we get into dark times or dark situations, God's light is always there to be found.

Jesus said, "I am the light of the world. *He who follows Me shall not walk in darkness, but have the light of life*" (John 8:12). Jesus came as a light to keep us from living in darkness. We have to trust that His light in us can never be put out.

Jesus came as the light of the world, but "men loved darkness rather than light, because their deeds were evil" (John 3:19). Those who are attracted to the dark do not want to give up their self-serving ways. We who love God want the light of Christ to expose anything in us that is attracted to the dark side in any way because that will keep us from being all we can be.

Jesus came to give you life in all its fullness. The enemy comes to rob and destroy you. Jesus came to give you His light and eternal life. The enemy comes to give you darkness and death. Choose to receive the gift of life *God* has for you.

When You Receive Jesus, He Gives You Life Forever with Him

This life is not all there is. You are going to live forever. Our soul will exist eternally, either in a stage of separation from God, or in eternal life with Him. Being separated from God is hell. That's what hell is. No one spoke about hell more than Jesus did. It's where the person who refused God will understand what God wanted to spare them from experiencing.

Heaven is being with God forever.

If you have received Jesus, one day you will have a resurrected body and eternal life with Him. The resurrection of Jesus guaranteed our own resurrection after we die. In many ways we are always being prepared for eternity. That's why we must choose heavenly rewards over earthly rewards. We must choose to love and serve God over all else.

The Bible says that when you die you will be instantly with the Lord. Jesus said He has prepared an eternal place for you. It's where nothing can harm you, where every need is supplied, where there is no more suffering, sickness, or struggle. He said, "Let not your heart be troubled; you believe in God, believe also in Me. *In My Father's house are many mansions; if it were not so, I would have told you. I go to prepare a place for you.* And if I go and prepare a place for you, I will come again and receive you to Myself; *that where I am, there you may be also*" (John 14:1-3).

What a magnificent promise the God of love has made to you.

The promise is that on your last day on earth, when you take your last breath, God will raise you up and bring you to your eternal home with Him. "God, who is rich in mercy, *because of His great love with which He loved us,* even when we were dead in trespasses, made us alive together with Christ (by grace you have been saved), and *raised us up together, and made us sit together in the heavenly places* in Christ Jesus" (Ephesians 2:4-6).

In light of all that, I would say for all of us who have received Jesus, the best is yet to come.

When Jesus raised Lazarus from the dead after he had been in the tomb three days, He said, "*I am the resurrection and the life. He who believes in Me, though he may die, he shall live.* And *whoever lives and believes in Me shall never die*" (John 11:25-26).

After He said that, He asked the people watching, "Do you believe this?"

He still asks the same question of us today.

Do you believe Him? Do you believe He is the resurrection and the life, and if you receive Him you will never die?

Was He crazy? Or is He the Son of God?

One of the best-known verses in the Bible by those who believe in Him is something Jesus said. "*God so loved the world that He gave His only begotten Son, that whoever believes in Him should not perish but have everlasting life*" (John 3:16).

The word "loved" here means a love that desires only the greatest good for us. The promise of life forever with Jesus cannot be minimized. God gave us Jesus because He loved us. He gave us Jesus so we could be restored into a relationship with Him. God's love is expressed to us by giving us His best.

When You Receive Jesus, You Receive More Than You Can Imagine

It takes a lifetime of growing in the Lord in order to truly understand all that Jesus did for you. I know this because I have been walking with Him for decades, and still He lets me see more and more of Him and the extent of the gifts He has given me in His sacrifice of love.

The thing is, we need spiritual eyes to see it all. The Bible says, "Eye has not seen, nor ear heard, nor have entered into the heart of *man the things which God has prepared for those who love Him.* But God has revealed them to us through His Spirit. For the Spirit searches all things, yes, the deep things of God" (1 Corinthians 2:9-10).

Jesus gives you an eternal fountain of living water that springs up inside you. It is from the indwelling Holy Spirit who provides a continual source of life.

When Jesus asked for a drink of water from the woman at the well in Samaria, she questioned why He, a Jew, would have anything to do with a Samaritan woman. Jesus told her that if she knew who He really was, she would have asked Him for *living* water (John 4:7-10).

He said, "Whoever drinks of this water will thirst again, but whoever drinks of the water that I shall give him will never thirst. *But the water that I shall give him will become in him a fountain of water springing up into everlasting life*" (John 4:13-14). Little did she know that this eternal fountain of life would come from His Spirit dwelling in her.

This fountain of life dwells in you by the same Holy Spirit.

Jesus referred to Himself as "the true bread from heaven" or "the bread of life." "Jesus said to them, 'Moses did not give you the bread from heaven, but My Father gives you the true bread from heaven. *The bread of God is He who comes down from heaven and gives life to the world.*' Then they said to Him, 'Lord, give us this bread always.' And Jesus said to them, '*I am the bread of life. He who comes to Me shall never hunger,* and *he who believes in Me shall never thirst*'" (John 6:32-35).

Without Jesus and the Holy Spirit, even if you believe in God, you will only have "a form of godliness" but you will be denying its power" (2 Timothy 3:5). You do not want faux godliness. You want the real deal. You want the true and living power of God to penetrate your life.

When we become so wrapped up in ourselves instead of wrapped up in Him, we forget the good news of what He came to earth to accomplish. That's why, even if we have walked with the Lord for a long time, we must continually be reminded of all we have been given through Him.

The birth of Jesus is one of the greatest events in all history. It is only surpassed by His death and resurrection. His entrance into the world had spiritual impact that shook the realm of darkness beyond what anything else could. He exposed the lies of the enemy with His truth. He gave us a way to forever be close to God. He secured our hope. He loved us that much.

We hear so much bad news today, but the truth about Jesus is always good news. And within the good news that we have in Him is the solution to all the bad news we see and hear.

He is the solution to all bad news in our lives.

And that is good news!

Prayer of *Love*

LORD, I realize I can never receive all You *have* for me until I understand everything You *did* for me. Thank You that You, "the ruler over the kings of the earth," loved me enough to wash me clean of all my sins by Your own blood (Revelation 1:5). Thank You that You are the living Word. You are my Savior. You have set me free from the consequences of my own sins, errors, mistakes, and ignorance. And You have made me to be a beloved child of God. Thank You that in You I find everything I need for life (1 Corinthians 8:6).

Thank You that You came "as a light into the world" so that I would never have to live in darkness (John 12:46). Thank You for Your Holy Spirit in me, for Your Word says that "if anyone does not have the Spirit of Christ, he is not His" (Romans 8:9). But You have given me Your Spirit when I received You, and He is the seal and sign that I am Yours and You are with me always. Because of all You have done for me, I will live eternally with You and no one can change that.

Thank You, Lord, that You share Yourself with me. You share Your love, peace, and power. You share Your Spirit and Your wholeness. You are the bread of heaven who feeds me life. You are the fountain of living water in me that never runs dry. You are the way, the truth, and the life. You are my foundation (1 Corinthians 3:11). You are the living Word and the door to eternal life. You are the good shepherd, and I hear the voice of Your Spirit leading me. Thank You that You are unchanging and I can forever depend on You (Hebrews 13:8).

In Jesus' name I pray.

Words of *Love*

In this the love of God was manifested toward us,
that God has sent His only begotten Son into the world,
that we might live through Him.

1 JOHN 4:9

I have been crucified with Christ;
it is no longer I who live, but Christ lives in me;
and the life which I now live in the flesh
I live by faith in the Son of God,
who loved me and gave Himself for me.

GALATIANS 2:20

God demonstrates His own love toward us,
in that while we were still sinners, Christ died for us.

ROMANS 5:8

In this is love, *not that we loved God, but that He loved us*
and sent His Son to be the propitiation for our sins.

1 JOHN 4:10

God did not send His Son into the world
to condemn the world,
but that the world through Him might be saved.

JOHN 3:17

4

Read God's
Love Letter to You

The greatest love story on earth is written in the Bible.

Actually, it *is* the Bible.

The entire Bible is a record of God's great love for us. One major sign of His love is that He gave us His Word.

After I received the Lord I started going to church to hear the pastor teach from the Bible, and the Scriptures came alive to me right away. At the pastor's encouragement I went out and bought my own Bible. I had opened up a Bible randomly a few times before but could not understand anything I read. Now, because I had opened my heart to the Lord, my spiritual eyes were opened as well, and I sensed God's love in every word.

It was far beyond anything I could have ever imagined.

For years I had been searching in the spirit realm for some kind of meaning for my life and a purpose for my existence. Now I saw that I had been plunging into the dark side—the wrong side of that realm—and I needed to come into the light. When I read about Jesus being the light of the world and there is no darkness in Him, I realized that the occult practices and false religions into which I had thrown myself were inhabited by another spirit. A dark spirit. The spirit of God's enemy. The opposite of God. Little did I know I had been consorting with the enemy of God.

When I separated myself from all that and walked into the realm of the God of infinite power, peace, and love, it was like night and day by comparison. I didn't conjure this up. I didn't imagine anything. It was unmistakable. It was more real than anything I had ever known, even more so than the fear and pain I had lived with for a lifetime. God's Word became a message of love and hope to me. I thought of it as a precious diamond, and every time I read it I found dazzling new facets. "I rejoice at Your word as one who finds great treasure" (Psalm 119:162). Each time I opened the Bible, I asked God to open my eyes to new depths of the truth I had not seen before. And He did.

The Bible became an unending source of life to me. I could hear God speaking to me by His Spirit on every page. And I felt His love each time.

When you enter into a close relationship with God, you will not only love *Him*, you will also love His *Word*. You cannot separate the two. God and His Word are one. That's because Jesus is the living Word of God, and God and Jesus are one. It was God's Holy Spirit who inspired the writers of the Bible and led them as they wrote it. The more you read God's Word, the more you will experience God's love.

Ask God to help you see and understand and sense His love for you in His Word as you read it. It has been written as His love letter to *you*. And the Holy Spirit will bring it alive to you every time.

There are countless ways God shows His love for you in His Word. What follows are only a few of them.

God's Word Gives You a Way to Make Life Work

God's laws and commandments are there because He loves us and He wants what is best for us. He gives us rules for our benefit.

Just like any loving parent, God gives us boundaries for our own good. Indulgent parents, who let their children do anything they want, raise kids with serious problems. You see it all the time. Children without boundaries are unstable. They get out of control. And they *feel* out of control. They misbehave without consequences, so they believe there are no consequences for breaking the rules. Parents who allow children to not follow the rules that exist for their protection don't do any favors for their children. People generally don't like children like that and don't want to be around them. And such children sense that they are not liked and that affects their personality. They develop less than optimal behavior, which leads to more rejection. This happens all because a parent does not love their children enough to give them rules with a requirement to obey them.

All children need to know what the boundaries are in order to survive and do well in life. We are God's kids, and we, too, need boundaries in order to survive and do well. Without God's Word, we will be influenced by the anti-Christ-formed *relativism* of the world more than the God-created *revelation* of the Holy Spirit.

Having absolutes in our life is freeing. Parents who love their children give them rules for their protection, and God does the same for *His* children. As a child of God, His laws free you to move into the plans and purposes He has for you. From His Word you find out what works and what *doesn't* work and never will. You don't have to wander down paths that will hurt you, rob you, ruin your life, and take you far away from the fulfillment and purpose God has for you.

That's why God's Word is His love letter to you.

God's Word Changes Your Heart and Mind

When you find true and lasting love, it is life-giving. Every time you read your loved one's messages, they touch you deeply and bring noticeable changes in your heart and soul. You cherish each word and search between the lines for every subtle meaning. The same is true of God's love letter to you. The more you read it and search for the deeper meanings, the more you understand His heart of love for you.

Every time you read God's Word with the idea that it is living and powerful, God will speak to your spirit and soul. If you invite Him to, He will touch you and change you. He will open your eyes to His truth and give you wisdom that will bring you into the realm of the truly wise. With such a strong lying spirit in the world today, God's Word gives you the truth. And we all need that in order to combat the lies of the enemy and stay on the right path.

"*The law of the* LORD *is perfect, converting the soul*; the testimony of the LORD is sure, *making wise the simple*; the statutes of the LORD are right, *rejoicing the heart*; the commandment of the LORD is pure, *enlightening the eyes*" (Psalm 19:7-8). You will love that His Word is true and His laws are right. Your heart will rejoice over their absolute dependability.

Jesus said, "It is written, 'Man shall not live by bread alone, but by every word that proceeds from the mouth of God'" (Matthew 4:4). We must be continually fed with God's Word every day because it is sustenance for our soul. We can't live well without it. It builds us up and changes us from the inside out.

Reading God's Word gives you clarity of mind and strength of soul. It *builds your faith*. It *provides guidance and direction*. It *encourages you* and *gives you hope*. It *comforts you* and *speaks to you about your value and worth and purpose*. It *gives you wisdom* and *understanding* and *knowledge*. It *helps you find* the *restoration and wholeness* God has for you.

God gave you His Word because He loves you. Always read it with that in mind.

God's Word Protects You and Guides You to a Place of Safety

God's Word is like an umbrella of safety for us, but we must know what it says in order to understand how to live under its protection. When we live opposite of what God's Word says, we come out from under that protective covering and can wander away from the life God has for us and get shot down by enemy fire.

When we have *God's Word guiding us* every day, when *we look to God for counsel* instead of the world, *we become solidly planted* where God's rivers of living water flow continuously into us. The Bible says of the person who delights in God's law, that he "*shall be like a tree planted by the rivers of water*, that brings forth its fruit in its season, whose leaf also shall not wither; and *whatever he does shall prosper*" (Psalm 1:3).

That's where you want to be—in that place of safety where you will not bear the consequences of disobedience. You will, instead, bear the fruit that nourishes and sustains you for life.

God's Word Is a Weapon of Warfare

God's Word is called "the Sword of the Spirit" for a reason: *His Word is a powerful weapon against the destructive powers of evil*. When we speak God's Word in the face of all that opposes us, every stronghold and threat is destroyed. *God's Word becomes a weapon against the enemy of our soul* when we stand strong in it and proclaim it. It assists us in disabling the enemy's plans for *our* destruction and allows us to concentrate on *his*.

As prayer warriors in God's army, we must keep in mind that our main *weapon* is the Word of God. It is not only part of our *protective* armor—the armor of God—but it is also a powerful offensive *weapon*. The enemy finds it very offensive. It is highly accurate, and if you are knowledgeable as to how to handle it as a weapon against the enemy, it is unfailing. If you aim correctly, it hits the target dead-on every time. The more skilled you are at using this powerful weapon, the greater advantage you have. In fact, the enemy cannot stand against it.

No soldier *resists* the enemy without his weapon. Neither does a soldier ever *attack* his enemy without the weapon he knows best how to use. He understands its capabilities, is completely familiar with it, and has practiced with it countless times. A soldier's weapons are always kept up to the highest standard and ready to use.

We must do the same with our spiritual weapons. We cannot wait until the enemy attacks to get familiar with our spiritual weapons. We have to know our weapons now so we are prepared for anything. The Word of God is our best weapon because it will always be exactly what we need in order to face every threat.

God is unchanging. That's because He doesn't *need* to change. He is perfect and complete. And His Word is the same. It is never irrelevant, no matter how much the enemy tries to make it seem that way. That's why you can claim promises in the Bible as absolute truth for your life.

When Jesus was tempted by the enemy in the wilderness, He resisted with Scripture specifically aimed at thwarting the enemy's temptations. Even the enemy knows that the Word of God is powerful and unfailing and he can never prevail against it. That's why he finally left Jesus alone. He could not entice *Him* with lies the way he can with far too many of *us*.

Our faith is extremely important in the effectiveness of this main weapon. And the more we train and practice in our knowledge and retention of the Word, the more our faith develops. The more diligently we *read* the Word, *quote* the Word, *pray* the Word, and *do* the Word, the stronger our faith will be. Our greatest weapon—God's Word—mixed with our faith will prove to be the invincible weapon we need in every situation.

When marksmen or snipers train with their weapons, they do it full time. They make practicing with their weapon a way of life so that it becomes part of who they are. In the missions they are sent on, they cannot afford to miss. They have to be dead-on every time. In that same way, our greatest weapon—the Word of God—must become part of who *we* are and not just something we read or hear. We must pore over it, read *all* of it, listen to it, understand it, quote it, and be able to stay solid in everything we know of it. That takes practice.

That's why it is important to read the Bible every day. Just as you need to spend time with the one you love, you need to spend time with the One who loves you more than anyone else could. Ask the Holy Spirit to make whatever you are reading that day come alive in a new and deeper way. The Holy Spirit will meet you there on the page and do exactly that. It's also crucial to etch some verses into your memory so that you can draw on them whenever you need to. If you have not done that before, start with just one.

For example, read: *"God has not given us a spirit of fear, but of power and of love and of a sound mind"* (2 Timothy 1:7). Say it again and again until it is part of your soul. Believe it. Quote it when you are afraid and feel powerless.

Weave Scripture into the fabric of your being.

Scripture that is part of you becomes an instrument of survival and warfare. It keeps you from doing the wrong thing. *"Your word I have hidden in my heart*, that I might not sin against You" (Psalm 119:11). And it gives you an unshakeable foundation when you face difficult situations. "Great peace have those who love Your law, and *nothing causes them to stumble"* (Psalm 119:165).

Satan tried to destroy Jesus when He was born by inspiring wicked King Herod to kill all the babies in Bethlehem. Thirty years later, when Jesus was baptized in water by John the Baptist, He was led into the wilderness by the Holy Spirit and Satan attacked Him again. This time Jesus' weapon against His enemy was Scripture.

No spiritual battle can be fought and won without our greatest weapon—the Word of God.

The Word is God-breathed. Each writer of the Bible was moved by the Spirit as his gifts and intellect were used by God to speak *through* him. The Word of God is so powerful that *it is a double-edged sword in our hands* (Hebrews 4:12). That means it is a *defensive* as well as an *offensive* weapon. All prayer warriors need both.

Some people say, "This part of the Bible was only for the Old Testament people, and that part was only for the disciples, and that other part was only for the Ephesians, and this was only for the Philippians…" and on and on until the entire Bible is explained away as just a history book. *Beware of anyone who wants to make the Bible into just a history book.*

The Bible is living and has power for today.

"All Scripture is given by inspiration of God, and is profitable for doctrine, for reproof, for correction, for instruction in righteousness, *that the man of God may be complete, thoroughly equipped for every good work"* (2 Timothy 3:16-17).

If you are a woman, please know that when the Bible says something like "man of God," as it does in the verse quoted above, it is not excluding women. It's like saying "mankind." And we all know that "mankind" includes women as well. So don't be concerned about that. I have heard as many concerns from men having a hard time over being called "the bride of Christ"—something all believing Christians are called in the Bible as Jesus prepares them for His return.

Every time you read God's Word, it will become more firmly planted in your mind and heart. The more solid you are in the Word, the more powerful it will be in protecting you. So put on the Word of God like a protective garment every morning. Let the love of God in it *live in you.*

God's Word is like a giant magnifying mirror. As we look into it every day, we not only see who God is, who Jesus is, and who the Holy Spirit is, we also see the truth about who *we* are. We also see who we are supposed to become.

Do you remember the wonderful promises I mentioned in the previous chapter, that God has given us so that we *"may be partakers of the divine nature"* (2 Peter 1:4)? They are contained in God's love letter to us. These promises—when we cling to them—lift us outside of our tendencies toward lust, sin, corruption, and a dead-end life, and enable us to share in God's holy nature.

God shares Himself with us because He loves us enough to want us to become more like Him.

The more I read the Bible, the more clearly I see one thing. That is, God means what He says. God's Word is never ineffective or irrelevant. He says of His Word that it will accomplish what He wants it to, and "it shall prosper in the thing for which I sent it" (Isaiah 55:11).

God promises that His love letter to you will produce great things in you beyond what you dream possible.

Prayer of *Love*

LORD, I thank You for Your Word. I know it is Your love letter to me because every time I read or speak it, I experience Your presence and love in a deeper way. It feeds my soul and makes my life rich. Help me to understand it better every day. "Open my eyes, that I may see wondrous things from Your law" (Psalm 119:18). Help me to know You in greater depth through it. Thank You that Your Word gives me truth and guidance for my life.

Thank You that Your Word is perfect and it changes me every time I read it. All Your laws and commandments are right and are there for my benefit as boundaries to keep me protected and safe. Thank You for the blessings I receive when I obey them. Your Word brings me peace and a sense of well-being. "Your testimonies also are my delight and my counselors" (Psalm 119:24). Help me to clearly hear You speak to me as I read Your Word.

Lord, I am grateful You always keep Your Word. I know I can faithfully take You at Your word and it will never fail me. You are the living Word, Jesus, and You have magnified Your Word above all Your name (Psalm 138:2). Etch it on my heart in a lasting and life-changing way. Weave it into the fabric of my being so that it becomes part of me. Help me to see Your love for me on every page.

In Jesus' name I pray.

Words of *Love*

The word of God is living and powerful,
and sharper than any two-edged sword,
piercing even to the division of soul and spirit,
and of joints and marrow,
and is a discerner of the thoughts and intents of the heart.

Hebrews 4:12

As the rain comes down, and the snow from heaven,
and do not return there,
but water the earth, and make it bring forth and bud,
that it may give seed to the sower and bread to the eater,
so shall My word be that goes forth from My mouth;
it shall not return to Me void,
but it shall accomplish what I please,
and it shall prosper in the thing for which I sent it.

Isaiah 55:10-11

Blessed is the man
who walks not in the counsel of the ungodly,
nor stands in the path of sinners,
nor sits in the seat of the scornful;
but his delight is in the law of the Lord,
and in His law he meditates day and night.

Psalm 1:1-2

This Book of the Law shall not depart from your mouth,
but you shall meditate in it day and night,
that you may observe to do according to
all that is written in it.
For then you will make your way prosperous,
and then you will have good success.

Joshua 1:8

The statutes of the Lord are right,
rejoicing the heart;
the commandment of the Lord is pure,
enlightening the eyes.

Psalm 19:8

5

Accept God's
Grace and Mercy

Many people don't fully receive God's love because they believe He is angry with them. They don't understand His grace and mercy and the extent of His complete forgiveness.

Before I learned how to receive God's love, I didn't think He was angry at me. I thought He didn't care enough about me to even *be* angry. I knew I had done many wrong things I wasn't proud of, and I could never go back and change all of that. I felt distant from God even though I tried everything I could to find a way to somehow connect with Him.

The various occult practices and Eastern religions I went into while searching for God held the promise of getting close to *a* god. At least, that's what I had heard and read, but they never came through. The spiritual realm I was searching in became more and more frightening as time went on. It proved to be anything but comforting. In fact, it was quite the opposite. With each new experiment into this spiritual world, I was left feeling more distant from *a* god than ever and increasingly disappointed, hopeless, and fearful.

It wasn't until I came to know the love of the one true God through receiving His unfathomable gift—Jesus' sacrifice of Himself—that I began to understand how God not only knew *who I was*, but He also cared about *who I would become*. He loved me and would never leave me to fend for myself as I had always done in the past. I had been searching for the smallest crumbs under God's table, and He had prepared a magnificent feast for me in His royal banquet hall.

Only then did I begin to comprehend God's amazing grace and mercy, and I was overwhelmed by the love of God igniting both.

Understanding God's Grace

Grace is divine assistance that is undeserved, given to us so that we can be restored to right relationship with God. It's a reprieve or exemption from having to pay the price for anything we've done that is not according to God's ways. It's a gift to us because Jesus already paid that price and we have received Him by faith (Romans 3:24).

By the grace of God we are saved from the consequences of choosing our own ways over God's. This is no small matter because it is not something we can do on our own (Ephesians 2:8). And it is not about conjuring up anything with positive thinking. I am not saying that happy, hopeful thoughts accomplish nothing. They are good, but you can only go so far with them. Our good thoughts don't save us from the eternal consequences of our actions. They don't get us into a right and close relationship with God. They don't bring us into eternity in God's presence. They can't.

We are not saved by doing everything perfectly. We are not capable of doing that anyway, no matter how hard we may try (Galatians 5:4-5). We are saved because *Jesus* did everything perfectly and we have chosen to receive Him by faith.

Grace is never given on the basis of what we've done. It is God's gift of love to us.

Imagine that you are locked up in prison and have been sitting on death row for years, waiting to die for a crime you committed. And there are eyewitnesses who saw you and testified against you.

But one day someone high up appears to you and says, "If you put your trust in me, I will see you are pardoned so thoroughly that it will be as if it never happened. You will be completely free from all past transgressions forever." How relieved and joyful would you be? How indebted would you feel toward that person?

This is what happens to you when you put your trust in Jesus.

Jesus came because of God's love. Grace means we don't have to work our way to God. We don't have to struggle to be good enough to be with Him.

He came to *us*.

To be with *us*.

He still comes to us, and to anyone who doesn't know Him, in order to draw us all to Himself by His love and grace.

God's "throne of grace" is where we can go in prayer anytime in order to find the help we need (Hebrews 4:16).

Understanding God's Mercy

God's mercy is unmerited favor, an act of divine compassion that does not give punishment that is warranted. In other words, God does not give us what we deserve. He could judge us but He doesn't. Instead, He shows mercy when we come to Him with a humble and repentant heart.

God is merciful because He is "gracious and full of compassion" (Psalm 111:4). His mercy is shown to you because He loves you and has compassion for you. Signs of His mercy are everywhere when you know and love Him. "The earth is full of the goodness of the LORD" (Psalm 33:5).

God promises us so many things in Scripture that assure us of His mercy. For example, He promised that the flood in Noah's time would never happen again. He promised that "'the mountains shall depart and the hills be removed, but *My kindness shall not depart from you*, nor shall My covenant of peace be removed,' says the LORD, who has mercy on you" (Isaiah 54:10).

He promised a rainbow to remind us.

In the same chapter, God spoke that famous promise to those who love and serve Him. "*No weapon formed against you shall prosper*" (Isaiah 54:17). That promise is a sign of God's compassion and mercy.

With so much evidence in the Word that God is merciful toward us, why do so many of us doubt that? Is it because we don't read His Word? Or if we do, we don't believe it? Or do we look at God's Word as just history instead of His love letter to us? Or do we identify more with being guilty than we do with being forgiven? Or do we see the things that are wrong in our life and blame God for them instead of seeking Him for the solution and thanking Him for all that is good? Or when we read God's Word, do we look for His judgment more than His love?

Whatever the reason, we must ask God to help us recognize His mercy shown toward us every day, for that is evidence of His great love for us.

God's Mercy Is a Sign of His Goodness and Love for Us

God's mercy is a sign of His constant, deep, unfailing love for us. We must "give thanks to the LORD, for He is good! For His mercy endures forever" (Psalm 136:1).

I had a pastor a number of years ago who was not only a great teacher and preacher of the Word, but He also clearly demonstrated the love of God. He was known for that. It was a great gift.

Pastor Tim had been a professional football player and had even won a Super Bowl with his team. He had the Super Bowl ring to prove it. He was a very large man, and I am certain he looked extremely ominous to the opposing team on the field. Let's just say that no one would want to be in his way after the football was hiked to the quarterback.

When he later became our pastor, we thought of him as a very large teddy bear because he consistently and abundantly exuded God's love to everyone in a joyful, sweet, and non-judgmental way.

I remember a specific teaching of Pastor Tim's on the goodness and mercy of God. He based it on the last verse of Psalm 23 that says, "Surely *goodness and mercy shall follow me all the days of my life*; and I will dwell in the house of the LORD forever." Pastor Tim had a great way of demonstrating the points of his teaching so we would not forget it. And I have never forgotten this one in particular.

Pastor Tim demonstrated that verse by asking two men from the congregation to stand just behind him—one on either side of him—and follow him wherever he walked and talked. He asked us to imagine that he was driving his car and he could see them in the rearview and side mirrors. He named one "Goodness" and the other "Mercy." He told us that as we walked through each day, we should imagine looking in the rearview mirror of our life and seeing the "Goodness" of God on one side and the "Mercy" of God on the other following us everywhere we went. And we could trust that they would always be there until we went to be with the Lord.

There's that mirror thing again. Only we are not seeing *ourselves*. Nor are we seeing our *past*. We are seeing God's *goodness* and *mercy* reflected in those mirrors.

Not long ago I was driving home after dark, and I noticed that the car that had followed me out of the parking lot was still behind me, making every one of the many turns I did. I began to become concerned, but every time I looked in the rearview mirror I said, "Thank You, Lord, that Your goodness and mercy will follow me all of the days of my life." The car followed me into my neighborhood, but as I turned right onto my street, the car turned left. The driver was probably just a neighbor, but that mental image of goodness and mercy gave me great peace.

God's goodness and mercy are signs of His deep and unfailing love for us that tell us He has our back.

Now every time I'm faced with difficulties, I recall that picture. What a comfort that is. I hope you, too, will imagine a rearview mirror and see God's goodness and mercy following you every day of your life—all because He loves you.

God Shows His Mercy by Forgiving Us

Because of God's grace we are forgiven of everything we have ever done wrong in the past once we receive Jesus. In fact, we are forgiven by God so completely that He does not remember it. "As far as the east is from the west, so far has He removed our transgressions from us" (Psalm 103:12). "I will be merciful to their unrighteousness, and their sins and their lawless deeds I will remember no more" (Hebrews 8:12). God wants us to forget about our failures too, and stop reliving them, rehashing them, and beating ourselves up over them.

When we forgive someone who has hurt us, we *choose* to let it go but usually don't forget it. We *decide* to not allow the remembrance of the grievance to cause us to be bitter, angry, or unforgiving but still remember.

When God forgives us, our sin against Him is completely erased from the records.

David said, "*Blessed is he whose transgression is forgiven, whose sin is covered. Blessed is the man to whom the LORD does not impute iniquity*" (Psalm 32:1-2).

What it means when "the LORD does not impute iniquity" is that our sin is not even put on our record.

Sin is an archery term meaning to miss the mark.

Iniquity means to be morally depraved.

Transgression means rebellion. *Not living God's way is rebellion against Him.*

Rebellion is the same as witchcraft—which means living in opposition to God's ways (1 Samuel 15:23).

Being released from the consequences of our transgressions and opposition to God's ways is one of the greatest acts of mercy God does for us.

However, once we have received Jesus and we *again* commit a transgression against the Lord, by His mercy He allows us to repent of that. God asks that we come to Him with a repentant heart and confess our transgression before Him. He already knows what we have done, but He wants to hear it from us and see that our heart is truly repentant.

God's mercy means that when you confess and repent of any transgression against God and decide to walk away from it and never intend to do it again, He forgives you.

If we do not repent before God, we become miserable and it ages us. It puts a burden on our mind, emotions, and shoulders we were not designed to carry. But when we confess our sins, He forgives us and releases us from the consequences of them.

The physical, mental, and emotional consequences of unconfessed sin take a major toll on us. David, who was no stranger to unrepentant sin, said, "When I kept silent, *my bones grew old* through my groaning all the day long. For day and night Your hand was heavy upon me; *my vitality was turned into the drought of summer. I acknowledged my sin to You*, and my iniquity I have not hidden. I said, 'I will confess my transgressions to the LORD,' and *You forgave the iniquity of my sin*" (Psalm 32:3-5). Even those who are the most rebellious and rejecting of the Lord's ways are forgiven when they repent before Him.

God doesn't forgive us because we deserve it; He forgives us because He loves us and is merciful toward us.

We all recognize the places in our heart that harbor thoughts, ideas, feelings, and attitudes that don't please God. We know ourselves all too well in that way. And we assume God is not pleased with us and therefore we don't deserve answers to our prayers.

But we have never *deserved* His blessings. That's what His mercy is all about.

We are forgiven of all past sins by His grace (Ephesians 1:7). After we receive Jesus, we are then forgiven of any subsequent sins because of His mercy.

God could just say, "I've forgiven you of all your past sins, but *that's it*. No more. I'm not doing this again. I expect you to be perfect from now on."

But it seems He knows us all too well.

God has set it up that the only way distance comes between us and Him is if we miss the mark He has for us—which we all do at one time or another—and then do not confess and repent of it. Our unconfessed sin sets consequences in motion, and God, who does not reward bad behavior, waits to bless us until we are sorry enough to turn to Him for forgiveness.

King David confessed and repented of his sinful affair with Bathsheba and the subsequent murder of her husband in order to hide his sin once she became pregnant. But David waited far too long to confess and repent. He had to be confronted about his choices by Nathan, a prophet of God. Once confronted, David went before God and said, *"Have mercy upon me, O God, according to Your loving kindness; according to the multitude of Your tender mercies, blot out my transgressions. Wash me thoroughly from my iniquity, and cleanse me from my sin"* (Psalm 51:1-2).

Even though David finally repented, he had still allowed the consequences of his unconfessed sins to be set in motion, which was the death of his and Bathsheba's child together.

Don't allow disobedience to God's ways to put up a wall between you and Him. Bring it to Him immediately with a repentant heart— meaning you are sorry about it and don't intend to do it again. God waits to answer our prayers until we get our heart right.

Sin has consequences. That is just the way it is. No one gets away without the consequences coming to fruition sooner or later. God's forgiveness in response to our repentance releases us from the consequences of our errors.

That's mercy.

God's Mercy Is Not Extended to Those Who Do Evil

Have you ever been afraid because of the evil around you? I know I have. The evil around me caused me to move out of a dangerous neighborhood into a safer one. Have you ever cried fervently before the Lord to protect you and your family and asked Him to remove you from the path of evil? I have done that countess times. "In my distress I called upon the LORD, and cried out to my God; He heard my voice from His temple, and my cry came before Him, even to His ears" (Psalm 18:6).

David said, "The pangs of death surrounded me, and the floods of ungodliness made me afraid" (Psalm 18:4). After his prayer was answered, he said of God, "He sent from above, He took me; *He drew me out of many waters. He delivered me from my strong enemy,* from those who hated me, for they were too strong for me. They confronted me in the day of my calamity, but *the LORD was my support.* He also brought me out into a broad place; *He delivered me because He delighted in me*" (Psalm 18:16-19).

Is that not the mercy of God?

That is what I believe God did for me and my family after I prayed for Him to move us to a safer place.

Evil people don't fear God. They are full of deceit and have no wisdom. They think about planning and doing wicked things day and night. They are never horrified by evil. In fact, they think highly of themselves when they do wrong.

David said of the wicked, "*There is no fear of God before his eyes.* For he *flatters himself in his own eyes,* when he finds out his iniquity and when he hates. The words of his mouth are wickedness and deceit; *he has ceased to be wise* and to do good. He devises wickedness on his bed; he sets himself in a way that is not good; he does not abhor evil" (Psalm 36:1-4).

God protects us when we make Him the safe place we turn to.

When David fled from Saul, he prayed, "Be merciful to me, O God, be merciful to me! For my soul trusts in You; and in *the shadow of Your wings I will make my refuge, until these calamities have passed by*" (Psalm 57:1).

David put his hope in God's mercy, and God protected him.

David said to God, "*You have delivered my soul from death. Have*

You not kept my feet from falling, that I may walk before God in the light of the living?" (Psalm 56:13).

If it is not our time to go, God keeps us from death. The psalmist said with faith in God's love and mercy, "I shall not die, but live, and declare the works of the LORD. The LORD has chastened me severely, but He has not given me over to death" (Psalm 118:17-18).

God's Mercy Helps Us Do What We Cannot Do on Our Own

When my children were small, they knew they would have certain privileges if they strictly obeyed the family rules. One of those rewards was going to a nice restaurant with us. My husband and I didn't have babysitters or family members around to take care of them for a few hours, and I wouldn't leave them with anyone unless I knew them well and completely trusted them.

Of course, we didn't take them out to nice restaurants if they were under the age of three—when they were still *all zeal and no wisdom*. But at three years old they knew their manners, especially toward the people serving us and other people around them in the restaurant. We were not about to inflict misbehaving children on others, and our kids were wise enough to know that.

Both children knew in advance that this night would be *all judgment and no mercy* if they misbehaved—at least for those 90 minutes. As a result of knowing that, they were perfect in their manners and soft spoken and mature in their conduct. They behaved because they wanted the privilege of going with us and eating the great food they loved so much.

Many times a person or a couple in the restaurant would come over to our table to comment on how well mannered our children were and how pleasantly surprised they were when our children conducted themselves more quietly and politely than many of the other adults there. They felt they had to say thank you.

God's mercy toward us, on the other hand, doesn't require us to be perfect in our behavior. That's why it is called mercy. It's His compassion toward us. Because He loves us He helps us to do the right thing. He helps us to do beyond what we can do on our own.

God's mercy is not a "get out of jail free" card that allows us to keep on disobeying His laws. There are consequences for violating God's laws, just as there are consequences for breaking the laws of a country. If there are no consequences, then there is either corruption in the system or there really are no laws. But if laws are upheld, the system is good.

God expects us to uphold His laws, and there are consequences when we don't. But He mercifully will help us to live His way when we ask Him to do so.

David said that the *faces of those who look to the Lord are radiant and unashamed* (Psalm 34:5). That is the same for the faces of children who are raised with guidance, godly discipline, and the love and mercy of the Lord. You can always tell the children whose parents love them enough to teach them what they need to know. Their faces reveal it.

God shows His great love and mercy in times of trouble. We have no idea how many times He has saved us from danger or death. "*The eye of the* LORD *is on those who fear Him, on those who hope in His mercy, to deliver their soul from death, and to keep them alive in famine*" (Psalm 33:18-19).

The best part about His goodness and mercy is that it allows you to dwell with Him forever. Jesus has prepared a place for you in eternity with Him where there is no disease, no crime, no evil, no sorrow, no fear, and no tears—once He wipes away all of yours, of course.

In the book of Revelation, John talks about what he saw regarding the end times. He said, "I saw under the altar the souls of those who had been slain for the Word of God and for the testimony which they held" (Revelation 6:9). We wonder, *Why does God allow those who love and serve Him to be murdered?* But we don't see the great reward waiting for them in heaven.

These are the people who had been killed because they were Christians and stood up for God, His Word, and their faith. They—the martyrs—were asking God how long it would be until He avenged their blood. They wanted God's justice to prevail.

God told them to rest a while longer until the remainder of those who would also be killed for their faith was fulfilled. There were going to be more who would be martyred, and apparently God was giving the perpetrators time to repent.

I don't know about you, but if it were up to me, I would immediately strike the people who killed my children with death, and certainly they would have no future in heaven. But not God. He is too merciful and loving for that. He loves us even when we sin against Him—even to the point of allowing them to destroy His most loyal servants and ardent believers, His beloved children who served Him faithfully to the end.

God loves us enough to wait for us to turn to Him so He can mercifully enable us to do what we cannot do on our own. That is, spend eternity with Him in heaven.

His grace and mercy are that deep.

He loves us that much.

Prayer of *Love*

LORD, thank You for Your grace and mercy, which I know are never-ending signs of Your unfailing love for me. They are gifts beyond comprehension. For it is You who redeems my life from destruction and crowns me "with lovingkindness and tender mercies" (Psalm 103:4). Thank You, Lord, that You "will perfect that which concerns me; Your mercy, O LORD, endures forever" (Psalm 138:8). Thank You that You care about the things I care about.

Thank You for Your forgiveness. I can't imagine the condition of my life and the state of my soul without it. I know that guilt is a killer and condemnation destroys. I am forever grateful that when I recognize my own error and bad choices that have led me to stray from Your ways, I can come to You with a humble and repentant heart and You not only will forgive me, but You remove my transgressions as far as the east is from the west (Psalm 103:12). "Do not remember the sins of my youth, nor my transgressions; according to Your mercy remember me, for Your goodness' sake, O LORD" (Psalm 25:7).

Thank You for Your grace that drew me to put my faith in You and allowed me to be saved from death and eternity without You. Thank You that Your grace is the great manifestation of Your love for me, and Your mercy keeps me from being punished as I deserve. Help me to keep myself in Your love, dwelling in the flow of Your mercy, even into heaven with You after I leave this earth (Jude 1:21).

In Jesus' name I pray.

Words of *Love*

By grace you have been saved through faith,
and that not of yourselves; it is the gift of God.

EPHESIANS 2:8

Let us therefore come boldly to the throne of grace,
that we may obtain mercy and find grace
to help in time of need.

HEBREWS 4:16

The LORD takes pleasure in those who fear Him,
in those who hope in His mercy.

PSALM 147:11

As the heavens are high above the earth,
so great is His mercy toward those who fear Him;
as far as the east is from the west,
so far has He removed our transgressions from us.

PSALM 103:11-12.

God, who is rich in mercy, because of His great love
with which He loved us,
even when we were dead in trespasses,
made us alive together with Christ
(by grace you have been saved), and raised us up together,
and made us sit together in the heavenly places
in Christ Jesus.

EPHESIANS 2:4-6

6

Recognize the Ways
God Loves You

Love is like a vapor.

We can't see a vapor, but we can sometimes sense the effects of it. For example, we can't see a gasoline vapor until it's ignited by a spark. Then we can definitely observe the effects of that. We don't see airwaves, but we recognize the manifestations of them when our cell phone rings or we turn on the radio. The more we learn about vapors and airwaves, the more we recognize that they are all around us.

The same is true about God's love. It's all around us, and He shows His love for us in countless ways, but often we don't see the manifestations of His love until He opens our eyes to them. It all begins when we receive the Lord. That turns on the receptors in our brain, heart, and spirit. Then, with each new recognition, there comes a burst of joy in us that is set off by our understanding of what has been there all along but we could not see it until that moment.

When we finally understand things about God's love that we have never before imagined, it is like an explosion in our heart detonated by the signs of it everywhere we look. We see it in His beautiful creation around us. We feel it in His grace and mercy extended to us. We recognize it in the things that happen for good in our life. His loving presence cannot be missed.

Even after our understanding of God's love for us is ignited, it will continue to explode in our heart like a blast to our senses every day, and each time it will touch us more deeply than the day before.

If you have never felt that, ask God to reveal the ways He shows His love to you. Even if you *have* felt His love in the past, ask Him to show you in new ways now. There is always more to learn and experience concerning God's love for you. Has He given you family, friends, relationships, healing, health, work, sun, and rain? I used to not appreciate rain until I was in a drought. Now every time it rains I praise God. I am not insensitive to those who have been in damaging floods, but even then, during frightening times when the forces of nature remind us how small and powerless we really are, God's love can still be seen in the way He protects us or provides for us. *There are so many things we do not appreciate in our life until we recognize God's love for us in them.*

Has God restored something in your life or removed something that needed removing? Has He protected you in ways you did not recognize at the time? Ask Him to show you what you have not yet recognized and thank Him when He does.

One of the primary ways we can identify God's love for us is by recognizing His promises to us in His Word and how He keeps them. What a comfort to know that everything He tells us is true and what He promises will come to pass.

When a parent promises a child that a particular thing will be done for him, that child does not forget. He *expects* it to happen. He *waits* for it. But if the parent forgets—or neglects to follow through—the child is hurt because he perceives it as a lack of love. Often, this disappointment is so deep that it can still be easily brought to mind decades later as an adult and the hurt is still there.

Keeping a promise to someone is a sign of love.

God always keeps His promises. And every promise is a sign of His love to us. We don't dictate to Him *when* or *how* these promises will be fulfilled. It is enough to know they will be.

What follows below are just a few of God's promises that are evidence of His great love for you.

God Promises That Nothing Shall Separate You from His Love

The love of God is constantly active and present. His love didn't just happen once. It's forever moving *in* you and *in your life*. You are never separated from His love. You can't be. His love is everywhere because God is love and He is everywhere. No matter how difficult life becomes for you, trust that His love is with you always. Only you can put a limit on how much of it you receive.

Paul said, "I am persuaded that *neither death* nor *life*, nor *angels* nor *principalities* nor *powers*, nor *things present* nor *things to come*, nor *height* nor *depth*, nor *any other created thing, shall be able to separate us from the love of God which is in Christ Jesus our Lord*" (Romans 8:38-39). This promise is not a small thing.

No matter what is going on in your life, nothing can separate you from God's love.

There is no *person* who can separate us from the love of God. "Who shall separate us from the love of Christ? Shall *tribulation*, or *distress*, or *persecution*, or *famine*, or *nakedness*, or *peril*, or *sword?*" (Romans 8:35). God blesses us even when our enemies are attacking us. Our life always overflows with His favor (Psalm 23:5).

This means that because of the love of God revealed to you through Jesus, you are able to conquer the obstacles in your life. He will restore your troubled soul and lead you in the way you should go (Psalm 23:3). Even if you have to walk through a place of great danger, you don't have to fear because God is with you. Even His correction of you when you get off the path is a sign of His love. His shepherd's crook will bring you back when you stray. That is a comforting sign of how much He loves you (Psalm 23:4).

His love for us broke the power of death and hell and gave us His Holy Spirit to be with us even into heaven. It means God is always on our side. "If God is for us, who can be against us?" (Romans 8:31).

God loves you completely, and there is nothing you can do to change that.

God Promises to Provide for You

Trusting that God will provide for you is not always easy, especially when you cannot even begin to see how what you need can possibly materialize. I have been in that place many times in my life, and God has come through in ways I could never have fathomed or dreamed of.

When you are convinced God loves you, and you look to Him with love and reverence in your heart, you will not lack anything. The Bible says, "Oh, taste and see that the LORD is good; blessed is the man who trusts in Him! Oh, fear the LORD, you His saints! *There is no want to those who fear Him...those who seek the LORD shall not lack any good thing*" (Psalm 34:8-10). What a remarkable promise to us. How can we *not* recognize God's love for us in those words?

God is a giver. It *pleases* Him to give us what we need.

Have you ever tried to give someone something you know they badly need but they will not accept it? It is very frustrating and kind of like a slap in the face. *Giving* is not the only sign of love; so is *receiving*. Jesus said, "It is your *Father's good pleasure* to give you the kingdom" (Luke 12:32). It's an affront to God to refuse to receive all He has for you. It's like saying, "I do not want or need what You have for me."

Jesus instructed us to "seek first the kingdom of God and His righteousness, and all these things shall be added to you" (Matthew 6:33). That means when we look to God, He will give us everything we need. When we don't receive all God has for us, it's like saying, "I'll get what I want by myself. I don't really need You." But God's Word says, "*Without faith it is impossible to please Him,* for he who comes to God must believe that He is, and that *He is a rewarder of those who diligently seek Him*" (Hebrews 11:6).

I love that Scripture. I have spoken it often in times of need, and it always brings great comfort to my heart. We must believe that because God loves us, He rewards us when we diligently seek Him.

God Promises to Transform You into His Image

When we walk with God, He promises to take us from glory to glory as we are transformed into His image. Don't you love that? He not only wants you to become more like Him, but He will help you do that. "We all, with unveiled face, *beholding as in a mirror the glory of the Lord*, are *being transformed into the same image from glory to glory*, just as *by the Spirit of the Lord*" (2 Corinthians 3:18). He says that if we keep looking to Him—like looking into a mirror—we will start seeing His image reflected back at us. The more we look to Him, the more we become *like* Him.

God also promises to take us from strength to strength when we look to Him to be strong in us. "Blessed is the man whose strength is in You...they go from strength to strength" (Psalm 84:5,7). When we choose to walk with God, we find our strength in Him (Psalm 29:11). When we look to Him, He shares Himself with us.

That is true love.

God Promises to Protect You

When we put our trust in God, He shields us from harm more than we know. The key is to put our trust in Him *all the time* and not wait for disaster to happen. Yet even when we put our trust in God and difficult things happen, we must not let our trust waver, for in the midst of trouble He will do great things in us and through us.

God is a safe place you can always run to when you are in danger. David said that the Lord "will be a refuge for the oppressed, *a refuge in times of trouble*" (Psalm 9:9). And He will never forsake anyone who seeks Him (Psalm 9:10). "For He will deliver the needy when he cries, the poor also, and him who has no helper" (Psalm 72:12). When we understand the condition of our soul without God's presence in our life, we see that we are poor and needy all the time.

This doesn't mean nothing troubling will ever happen, but it won't *keep on* happening. And God will do great things in the midst of it. *"He sets the poor on high, far from affliction,* and makes their families like a flock...Whoever is wise will observe these things, and they will understand the lovingkindness of the LORD" (Psalm 107:41,43).

God's promise to protect us doesn't mean we can test Him by taking foolish chances. Satan tried to tempt Jesus to test God's love for Him. He took Jesus up to the pinnacle of the temple and said, "If You are the Son of God, throw Yourself down. For it is written: 'He shall give His angels charge over you,' and, 'In their hands they shall bear you up, lest you dash your foot against a stone'" (Matthew 4:6). Even Satan knows the Word of God enough to use what we *don't know* against us. Jesus answered him by quoting the Word, saying we are not to put God to a test (Matthew 4:7 NIV).

When I lived in a "strong city" with danger all around, God protected me and my family. I used to declare the following verse often: "Blessed be the LORD, for He has shown me His marvelous kindness in a strong city!" (Psalm 31:21). But I never tested God on that. I didn't go out walking alone at night. I didn't send my children to play in the front yard near the street. I didn't open my door to strangers, and I taught my children to never do that as well.

God knows what is going on all around us even when *we* don't. He knows the plans of the enemy for our lives. We must *trust* God and not *test* God in these things. When we look to the Lord to protect us, He makes certain *His* plans for us succeed and not the enemy's. But we don't hang around the enemy and entertain his suggestions just to see how well God is protecting us.

God didn't say we would never fall. He said *when* we do stumble, we will be upheld by Him. "The steps of a good man are ordered by the LORD, and He delights in his way. *Though he fall, he shall not be utterly cast down; for the LORD upholds him with His hand"* (Psalm 37:23-24).

That means without God it could have been a lot worse.

The angel of the Lord "encamps" around those who reverence God and delivers them (Psalm 34:7). Don't you love that promise? Wouldn't you like to look into the spirit realm for even a moment to see the angel of the Lord encamping around you? But God wants us to live by faith and not by sight—faith that He protects whom He loves and who also love Him.

Enjoying the presence of God in the daytime, living in the safety and peace He gives us, allows us to sleep better at night.

God Promises to Hear Our Prayers and Answer Them

Think of how much you love your child or children—or whomever you love most in this world. Well, God loves you even more because He has greater capacity to do so. He doesn't have the capability to not love because He *is* love. He cannot be what He is not. Jesus said, "If you then, being evil, know how to give good gifts to your children, how much more will your Father who is in heaven give good things to those who ask Him!" (Matthew 7:11). He answers our prayers because He loves us.

Keep in mind, though, that He doesn't promise to answer our prayers exactly the way we prayed them, but rather according to His will (1 John 5:14-15). Every promise of God has a condition that must be met. The most common conditions are that we must have faith in Him, and live His way, and believe His Word.

Whenever we are overwhelmed, we must remember that God is not. We must look to Him at those times and stop focusing on our situation. That doesn't mean we live in denial about it. "Denial religion" is not faith. We don't have to pretend our circumstance have not happened, as some do. We must be honest with God about our fears. David prayed, "Hear my cry, O God; attend to my prayer. From the end of the earth I will cry to You, *when my heart is overwhelmed; lead me to the rock that is higher than I*" (Psalm 61:1-2).

Jesus said, "Whatever things you ask in prayer, *believing, you will receive*" (Matthew 21:22). All we have to do is believe Him—that He is the Son of God and that He loves us and wants to answer our prayers. It is not our faith that does it. We are not having faith in our faith, as if we have anything to do with it. We have faith that He hears us and will answer our prayers according to His will, and that we are the recipient of His love when we pray.

God Promises to Deliver Us from Fear

The Bible tells us about the joy, blessing, and happiness of all those who fear God. *Fearing God means to reverence Him and fear what life would be like without Him.*

"Oh, how great is Your goodness, which You have laid up for those who fear You… *You shall hide them in the secret place of Your presence from the plots of man*" (Psalm 31:19-20). He blesses those who reverence Him.

That is *godly* fear.

The other kind of fear is not of the Lord. It is a spirit that can torture us if we allow it to grow in our heart. "God has not given us a spirit of fear, but of *power* and of *love* and of a *sound mind*" (2 Timothy 1:7).

The *power* is God's power, which He shares with us.

His *love* comforts us and takes away our fear.

A *sound mind* means having clarity of thought, good judgment, and the ability to make wise decisions and choices. It means having self-control and not being out of control in our actions and behavior. It means having the mind of Christ.

Beside that powerful verse from 2 Timothy above, Psalm 34 has always been my go-to place in the Bible when I need God's Word to quickly take away fear and insecurity. The entire psalm is an encouragement. A fixer of the heart. A readjustment of the attitude.

In these verses David vows to worship God continually and invites others to do the same. He said. "*I sought the LORD, and He heard me, and delivered me from all my fears*" (Psalm 34:4). David chose to seek God, and God answered by delivering him from every fear he had.

Just reading that psalm gives me peace in my heart. I know it will do the same for you as well.

God Promises Us the Crown of Life When We Resist Temptation

God knows we cannot be perfect, so He asks us to look to Him for strength to stand strong against any temptation to violate His ways for our life.

God promises to enable us to do things we cannot do without Him, but we have to declare our dependency upon Him. When we do, there are rewards for living His way.

James, the brother of Jesus, said, "*Blessed is the man who endures temptation*; for when he has been approved, *he will receive the crown of life which the Lord has promised to those who love Him*" (James 1:12). The crown of life is no small thing. This verse is talking about when we are in heaven with the Lord. There are rewards in eternity we will forfeit if we continue to allow ourselves to fall into temptation instead of resisting it. We all have access to the power and strength to resist temptation when it comes if we run to God at the first inkling of it and depend on *His* strength and power to do so.

That means when we go through hard times—and we don't lose faith and end up doing something stupid or faithless or selfish—the experience will cause us to depend on God so completely we will see that we need nothing else but Him.

James said, "*Count it all joy* when you fall into various trials, knowing that the *testing of your faith produces patience.* But let patience have its perfect work, *that you may be perfect and complete, lacking nothing*" (James 1:2-4).

If we recognize the testing of our faith when temptation presents itself and we run to God, we can have joy in the process of resisting the enemy of our soul. If we depend on God to work in us and perfect us, we will see that everything we need can be found in Him.

The sooner we learn that, the better off we will be.

God Promises That You Have a Good Future Ahead

Because God loves you, He promises you hope and a good future. Listen to what He says about you in His Word.

> I know the thoughts that I think toward you, says the LORD, thoughts of peace and not of evil, *to give you a future and a hope.* Then you will call upon Me, and go and pray to Me, and I will listen to you. And *you will seek Me and find Me, when you search for Me with all your heart (Jeremiah 29:11-13).*

God promises to us a great future with Him, but we must seek Him and search for Him with our whole heart. When we don't do that, He shows love for us in His discipline and correction. It means He loves us enough to care how we turn out. "For whom the LORD loves He chastens" (Hebrews 12:6). He said, "As many as I love, I rebuke and chasten" (Revelation 3:19).

In addition to the promises that reveal His love to us all the time, ask God to demonstrate the ways He shows His love to you personally. Has He spared you from something? Connected you with people you need to know? Put beauty in your path in amazing ways? Answered your prayers? Worked something out for good? Enabled you to recover? Helped you through a tough time? Spoken to your heart? Given you a sense of His presence? Gifted you with unexpected peace in the midst of crisis? Surprised you with joy? Spared you from something bad? Met you at your greatest point of need? Provided for you unexpectedly? Shown you things in His creation that have delighted you?

Whatever it is, thank God for His love whenever you see or remember it. Tell Him how much His love means to you. Ask Him to enable you to recognize and receive His love for you in every way. For it is the love of God you receive that will affect how you express your love for Him—and how consistently you show love to others.

Prayer of *Love*

LORD, thank You that Your Word promises to those in need that "in the days of famine" we will "be satisfied" (Psalm 37:19). I don't have to fear not having enough, and I can trust that because You are my Lord, I will not want for anything (Psalm 23:1). Thank You that You have a place of rest for me where there is fruitful abundance (Psalm 23:2). Thank You that You will not withhold any good thing from those who live Your way (Psalm 84:11).

Many of the promises in Your Word assure me that You will provide for me—all because You love me. I know Your ways are perfect and You have proven Your Word time after time. I know You will always be a shield to me because I trust in You (Psalm 18:30). Thank You that "*You have been a shelter for me, a strong tower from the enemy. I will abide in Your tabernacle forever; I will trust in the shelter of Your wings*" (Psalm 61:3-4). "I will both lie down in peace, and sleep; for You alone, O LORD, make me dwell in safety" (Psalm 4:8).

Thank You, Lord, that You are "a God near at hand" and "not a God afar off" (Jeremiah 23:23). "You have also given me the shield of Your salvation; Your right hand has held me up, Your gentleness has made me great" (Psalm 18:35). "You, O God, have heard my vows; You have given me the heritage of those who fear Your name" (Psalm 61:5). "You have put gladness in my heart" (Psalm 4:7). Help me to recognize Your love for me in Your Word and in all the ways You reveal Your love for me every day.

In Jesus' name I pray.

Words of *Love*

Show Your marvelous lovingkindness by Your right hand,
O You who save those who trust in You
from those who rise up against them.

PSALM 17:7

There is no fear in love; but perfect love casts out fear,
because fear involves torment.
But he who fears has not been made perfect in love.

1 JOHN 4:18

We know that all things work together for good
to those who love God,
to those who are the called according to His purpose.

ROMANS 8:28

The LORD will command His lovingkindness
in the daytime,
and in the night His song shall be with me—
a prayer to the God of my life.

PSALM 42:8

Your lovingkindness is before my eyes,
and I have walked in Your truth.

PSALM 26:3

7

Know What God's Love
Will Do in Your Life

~~~~~~

If God is love and God is everywhere, that means we are surrounded by His love at every moment. Why, then, don't we
always feel it? It's because the degree to which we sense God's love
for us depends on our *expectation of* Him and our *response to* Him.

Some people accept God's love wholeheartedly the moment they
have an understanding of who He is and what He has done. Others
are slower to open up to Him. They don't *expect* Him to love them
the way He does, so they don't respond to His hand on their life
with complete trust.

For example, one woman I have been friends with for decades
was a hundred percent sold out to God as soon as she gave her life to
Jesus and never looked back. She received His love completely and
didn't doubt it for a moment. I saw this with my own eyes and was
always amazed. And then I had another close friend who received
the Lord but could never fully accept that He loved her.

I knew both of them for years, and they were not extreme cases
of great or little faith, yet what was the difference between them?
After talking with countless women about this very subject over the
years, I believe these two friends actually represent many more people than we realize.

The first friend, who loved the Lord and received His love immediately, came from a very loving family. Their care and affection for
one another was clear and unmistakable. Unfortunately, she experienced great tragedy in her life when both of her parents were killed
in a car accident. But even though she was just a young woman at
that time and had to take on the role of a parent for her young sis-
ter and brother, I have never seen anyone so fully committed to the
Lord and who received His love as thoroughly as she did. I believe
that because she had *been* loved and *felt* loved, she knew how to
receive love.

The second friend had been raised by a seriously alcoholic mother
and a father in denial. Her hurts were deep and she never felt loved. I
led her to the Lord a year after I received Him myself, and although
she loved God she had a hard time believing He loved *her*. She read
the Bible. She prayed and went to church, yet she could not receive
His healing love completely. She married a man who was unloving and unaffectionate because of his own loveless childhood. She
died not many years later, and I believe her unmended broken heart
weakened her so that she did not have the strength to recover when
she became ill. She did not love herself and could never fully believe
God loved her either. She didn't find the healing and wholeness God
had for her because she had no expectations about His restoring love
on her behalf. Therefore, her response to Him was, at best, weak.

As for me, I was somewhere in between those two. I felt unloved
as a child. I felt unloved as an adult. But when I received the Lord,
I felt His love in the church, in the pastor's office with my friend
where I received Him, and in the believers around me. I believed
God was the God of love, but I didn't fully believe He really loved
me. I sensed His love from others, but I thought of it as more of an
overflow from those who actually were, in fact, loved.

Though it took awhile to truly believe God loved *me*, I did get
there eventually. It took trusting His Word to be a love letter to
me. And it took a lot of prayer—alone with God as well as praying

together with others. (More about this kind of healing in the following chapters.)

There is so much God wants to do in each of our lives, but all of that will be hindered as long as we don't trust His love for us. We will never view His love correctly until we understand Him. Unless we understand that God is love and we look for manifestations of His love in His Word and in our life, we won't recognize them as such, and so we will not rest in His love as we should.

It's important to know what God's love can and will accomplish in you. There are wonderful things He does, and *can* do, and *will* do in all of us. If we open up to His love working in us and receive it fully, communicate often with Him in prayer, receive from Him daily in His Word, and ask Him to reveal His love to us and help us choose to believe Him, then we will grow in His love every day and be able to receive all He has for us.

Be on the lookout for the healing and restoring work of God's love in you. His love is there for you because *He* is there for you.

What follows are just a few examples of how God's love will work in you that need to be kept in your mind.

God Will Calm the Storms in You and in Your Life

The storms in me were unending until I surrendered myself to the Lord at what was—and I am sure always will be—the lowest point in my life. When I received the Lord, I had no idea how much I was really receiving. It was a process to learn and understand it all.

When I went for Christian counseling and the counselor, Mary Anne, prayed for me, I was set free of the depression, anxiety, and deep sadness I had lived with for as long as I could remember. I felt the physical manifestation of those things being lifted off of my shoulders, and I was undeniably different afterward.

At that time I asked Mary Anne if I should change my name from Stormie to something normal because I never liked being teased about it growing up. I always wanted a simple name like everyone else that no one would make fun of or question.

I remember one time in church when we were asked by the pastor to form a circle of three to five people around us and introduce ourselves and pray for one another. When I introduced myself to the circle of four others, the only other woman in the group said loudly and insensitively, "What kind of parent would name their child a horrible name like that?"

I had only known the Lord a short time and had not yet had much emotional healing. As a result, her seemingly angry outburst hurt and embarrassed me, and I didn't know how to respond. I stood silent, hoping I would not cry and that someone else would speak.

My name always brought unwanted attention to me, and I didn't think it was a positive thing. But when I asked Mary Anne if I should change it, she immediately said, *"No, your name will be a testimony to how God calms the storms in our life."*

And it has been. Little did I ever dream how many storms God would calm. Actually, He calmed them all.

The truth is that His love can do great things in each of us. We have no idea. It's beyond what we can even imagine. I never dreamed of all that God has done in me. I am still amazed every day. So many people end their lives because they cannot picture a future for themselves worth living. They cannot see a way out of their pain and trouble. They are unable to imagine love so great that God would reach down and touch them with transformation.

I know from experience that people don't really want to die; they just can't see any other way out of their misery. I know that pain. And I believe that part of the enemy's plan for our destruction is to blind us to the truth of how much God loves us and all that He has for us in our future.

The Bible says of those who are in a storm in their lives that "their soul melts because of trouble...they cry out to the LORD in their trouble, and He brings them out of their distresses. *He calms the storm, so that its waves are still.* Then they are glad because they are quiet; so He guides them to their desired haven" (Psalm 107:26, 28-30).

God not only calms the storm but also gets us where we need to go.

Jesus calmed the storm for His disciples when they were out in a boat in the middle of the raging sea. They feared capsizing, but He walked on water toward them, and when He saw they were afraid He calmed the storm. He didn't silence the storm because He, too, was afraid, but because He loved them.

God loves you so much that He will not only save you from destruction but also not leave you the way you are. He begins the process of transformation in you immediately when you invite Him to do so.

Whatever storm is raging in your life, ask God to calm it for you. He will.

He loves you that much.

God Will Bring Good Out of Bad Situations

We can all find ourselves in troubled times because of a wrong decision we have made, or a lack of judgment on the part of others, or something bad that happens to us through no fault of our own and yet we are left to pay the consequences. I have learned over the many years I have walked with God that no matter how impossible a situation seems to me, even if I don't see how it can ever be overcome, it's not impossible for Him. I know to trust Him no matter what is happening.

Never forget that *with God, nothing is impossible.* That's because He is the God of the impossible to those who believe in Him. Jesus Himself said, "With God all things are possible" (Matthew 19:26).

It can't get any clearer than that.

God can turn the wilderness of our lives into a fruitful existence when we live His way. The Bible says of God, "*He turns a wilderness into pools of water*, and dry land into watersprings" (Psalm 107:35)

One of the greatest assurances of God's love is that He will work everything out for good when we love Him and live in the plans and purposes He has for us (Romans 8:28). The earlier verses before that are talking about praying. It seems to me that we can't expect to see everything in our life work out for good if we do not love God enough to pray and seek His help and His will.

God Will Always Be with You When You Are with Him

God knows you better than you know yourself. He always knows where you are and sees what you are doing and all that is happening to you, but He responds to your prayers. He will stay out of your life if you don't invite Him into it. It's the old "free will" thing again. If it's your will to exclude Him from your life, then you forfeit the blessings and benefits He has for you.

David said, "O LORD, *You have searched me and known me. You know my sitting down and my rising up; You understand my thought afar off. You comprehend my path* and my lying down, and *are acquainted with all my ways*... You have hedged me behind and before, and *laid Your hand upon me*" (Psalm 139:1-5).

God watches over you.

His hand is always on you, whether it feels like it at the moment or not. If you will acknowledge Him every day, He will lovingly lead you in the way you should go. Even when it seems your prayers are not answered, don't doubt that God hears you and sees your circumstances. Keep praying and looking to Him.

In the beginning of my walk with God—before I found freedom from depression, anxiety, and emotional pain—I valued being in church and sensing His presence in the worship and Bible teaching. I especially looked forward to the prayer time when the congregation broke into those small circles and prayed for one another. Even though it frightened me to pray out loud for others, I needed prayer so desperately I was willing to do whatever it took—even if it meant I might appear to look stupid—because it was the only time anyone ever prayed for me.

One Sunday morning when I was in church, the people around me all turned and separated into prayer groups, but I was left standing alone. I started crying because I was in such emotional pain that day I could not even speak to ask anyone to let me in their circle. But God sent a man who reached in from the aisle to pray with me. I don't know who he was and I never saw him again. I don't even know how he saw me because I was surrounded by people and none of *them* saw me. I felt invisible. I *was* invisible. But not to God. *He* saw me and sent someone to pray with me.

When you feel you will break down if you even try to talk to someone about your problems, don't allow yourself to be isolated. Ask God for help. I know He will do the same for you as He did for me if you cry out to Him.

David said, "Where can I go from Your Spirit? Or *where can I flee from Your presence?* If I ascend into heaven, You are there; if I make my bed in hell, behold, You are there. If I take the wings of the morning, and dwell in the uttermost parts of the sea, *even there Your hand shall lead me,* and Your right hand shall hold me" (Psalm 139:7-10). God never leaves us once we receive Him. We have to believe that every day.

Even when you are deserted by others, God will never forsake you. David said, "*When my father and my mother forsake me, then the* LORD *will take care of me*" (Psalm 27:10). If you have been rejected or deserted by your family, God is your family now and He will never leave you. He is always there for you unless you exclude Him from your life. Even then it is not that He leaves you, but His power in your life manifests only when you trust Him.

The Spirit of God came upon Azariah the prophet, and he said to King Asa, "*The* LORD *is with you while you are with Him. If you seek Him, He will be found by you; but if you forsake Him, He* will forsake you" (2 Chronicles 15:2). That is a serious truth. God is always with us, but He does not intervene in our lives unless He is invited to do so.

The problem is, *we* are not always with *Him*.

We too often allow diversions, temptations, secret idols, preoccupations, and interests into our life. Some people who neglect to be *with Him* are the first to fault Him for not doing what they want. They blame Him for things that happen when they should have brought it to Him in prayer. They should have trusted His love for them and His work in their life.

Don't let that happen to you.

Tell God you are with Him every day, and thank Him that He is always with you.

God Will Be Your Hiding Place from Trouble

Jesus didn't say we would never have problems. He said He would be with us in them. The Bible assures us that "many are the afflictions of the righteous, but *the LORD delivers him out of them all*" (Psalm 34:19).

When we do good and not evil, God delivers us from trouble. When our hearts are broken, God is especially near to us. When we are humble, God saves us. "The righteous cry out, and the LORD hears, and delivers them out of all their troubles. *The LORD is near to those who have a broken heart,* and saves such as have a contrite spirit" (Psalm 34:17-18).

God's love for you gives you security. David said, "[God] heard my cry. *He also brought me up out of a horrible pit,* out of the miry clay, and set my feet upon a rock, and established my steps…Blessed is that man who makes the LORD his trust" (Psalm 40:1-2,4).

When you make God your hiding place, He will surround you and you will be hidden in Him. "*You are my hiding place; You shall preserve me from trouble*" (Psalm 32:7). No matter what comes upon your life like a flood, God will protect you by lifting you out of it or taking you through it. "Surely in a flood of great waters they shall not come near him" (Psalm 32:6). That's why it is important to listen for the quiet voice of God's Spirit speaking to your heart and telling you what to do.

When you are overwhelmed by troubles, cry out to the Lord and say, "Hear my prayer, O LORD, and let my cry come to You…incline Your ear to me; in the day that I call, answer me speedily…My days are like a shadow that lengthens, and I wither away like grass" (Psalm 102:1-2,11). God always hears the prayers of anyone whose heart is humble, honest, and right in His sight.

You will never regret putting your trust in God. David said of the Lord that *"none of those who trust in Him shall be condemned"* (Psalm 34:22). Putting your trust in God does not mean demanding that He do what you ask. It's telling Him the desire of your heart and waiting on Him for the answer. I have found that the more time you spend with God in prayer, the more certain He will respond to a quick prayer when something sudden happens and there is little time for anything more.

God Will Not Forsake You in Old Age

God will never put you out to pasture. Isn't that good to know? Only the world does that. Only the world dares to say, *You don't have value after a certain age or a certain strength of body.* In God's eyes you are never over the hill. You are always valuable to Him. He never stops having a purpose for your life, and He will see to it that you bear fruit until He calls you home to be with Him.

The psalmist prayed, *"Do not cast me off in the time of old age; do not forsake me when my strength fails"* (Psalm 71:9). He also prayed, "Now also when I am old and grayheaded, O God, do not forsake me, until I declare Your strength to this generation, Your power to everyone who is to come" (Psalm 71:18).

If you are still breathing, God has a purpose for your life. And there are people He will put in your life who need to hear the truth and good news He has for them. And you will be the one He has chosen to deliver His message and His love.

God Will Empower You to Live the Life He Has for You

Another wonderful thing about God is that He doesn't just leave us down here on earth to fend for ourselves. He doesn't say, "Don't call Me, I'll call you." He doesn't tell us, "Good luck. Call Me if you absolutely can't find any other solution."

Quite the opposite, actually.

A sign of God's great love for us is that He empowers us to do what we cannot do on our own. Knowing that truth gives us confidence to face seemingly impossible situations in our life.

Don't let the world, the government, the press, or godless people tell you what your future is or is not. *God* has given you a future and a hope. *God* says He will bless those who look to Him. Despite the troubles we see around us, this can be the best time of our lives if we correctly see what God is doing. He gave Joseph and Egypt seven years of plenty *before* the seven years of famine. He provided for His people in both seasons.

God will provide for you in every season of your life too. In the rough times as well as the good times. You don't have to fear the future because in the presence of God's love all fear is evaporated. His perfect love for you will cast out all fear in your life (1 John 4:18).

God says, "I am the LORD, I do not change" (Malachi 3:6). That means He doesn't change His mind about you. The apostle Paul said, "Jesus Christ is the same yesterday, today, and forever" (Hebrews 13:8). Nothing in Scripture says that what Jesus did was only for the time He was here. Jesus said, "Most assuredly, I say to you, *he who believes in Me, the works that I do he will do also*; and greater works than these he will do, because I go to My Father" (John 14:12).

The same Holy Spirit who works in our lives and in the world today worked in the miraculous life of Jesus. The Holy Spirit is the same as well.

Paul prayed for the Ephesians that they would "be strengthened with might through His Spirit in the inner man" (Ephesians 3:16). He wanted them to receive Christ in their heart so His Holy Spirit would live in them, and they would be "rooted and grounded in love" so that they could comprehend *"what is the width and length and depth and height"* of God's love (Ephesians 3:17-18). He wanted them to "know the love of Christ which passes knowledge" and be filled with the fullness of God (Ephesians 3:19).

Paul prayed that they would build on a foundation of God's love—not just the *knowledge* of God's love but the *experience* of it. We ought to pray the same for ourselves as well.

Because God loves you, you can have peace beyond comprehension. The peace of God can always be yours. Jesus said, "Peace I leave with you...*Let not your heart be troubled, neither let it be afraid"* (John 14:27). He said, "These things I have spoken to you, that in Me you may have peace. *In the world you will have tribulation; but be of good cheer, I have overcome the world"* (John 16:33).

Jesus overcame the world and now empowers you to do the same.

The life God has for you is a fruitful life.

Jesus described Himself as the true vine. He said when we receive Him, we become branches that are grafted into Him. He warned us that we cannot bear fruit unless we stay closely connected to Him as our lifeline. He said, *"He who abides in Me, and I in him, bears much fruit; for without Me you can do nothing"* (John 15:5). If we are not bearing good fruit in our life, it's because we are not plugged into the true vine.

Jesus also said, "My Father is the vinedresser. Every branch in Me that does not bear fruit He takes away; and *every branch that bears fruit He prunes, that it may bear more fruit"* (John 15:1-2). In order for a branch to bear fruit it must be pruned. That means it must be cut back so the dead or unproductive areas are taken away and it can become stronger. We cannot prune ourselves as well or as thoroughly as *He* can. We need Him to see all that is dead in us that has to be cut off. He will get rid of whatever keeps us from producing more fruit.

If we choose to not walk with God and continue on in that way, we are then cut off from our life source. But if we stay connected to Him, or come back to Him in repentance, then our prayers are answered. Jesus said, "*If you abide in Me, and My words abide in you, you will ask what you desire, and it shall be done for you*" (John 15:7).

Abiding in the Lord is the key to having your prayers answered.

Jesus saves you *from much*, and *to much*, for a purpose. He wants you to bear good fruit. And because He loves you, He will enable you to do that.

God loves you more than you know. You can choose to open up your heart and receive it. When you do that, your life will never be the same. And I assure you that you won't want it to be.

Prayer of *Love*

LORD, I am amazed at what You *can* and *will* do in me because You love me. Help me to understand the expanse of Your reach into my life. Enable me to remember this when I am in the middle of a storm and need You to bring calm (Psalm 107:28-29). Thank You that You can turn a wilderness into a pool of refreshing water (Psalm 107:35). Thank You that You always see me and know where I am. I am grateful that because I have invited You to be Lord over my life, Your hand is always upon me. Thank You that because I am with You, You are always with me.

I have made You my hiding place from trouble, and I know You will surround me "with songs of deliverance" (Psalm 32:7). Thank You that when I am afraid I can run to You and You will deliver me from all my fears (Psalm 34:4). Only You can bring good out of bad situations when I submit them to You. I pray You will bring great things out of all that is difficult and troubling in my life.

I am grateful that because You love me, there is no place I can be that Your Spirit is not with me (Psalm 139:8-10). Thank You that You will never leave or forsake me, and even in old age I will always have a great purpose. Help me to abide in You so that I will always bear good fruit in my life. I know that without You I can do nothing good and lasting. Thank You that because You love me You will give me everything I need to live the life You have for me.

In Jesus' name I pray.

Words of *Love*

There is no fear in love; but perfect love casts out fear,
because fear involves torment.
But he who fears has not been made perfect in love.

1 JOHN 4:18

The wicked is ensnared by the transgression of his lips,
but the righteous will come through trouble.

PROVERBS 12:13

Likewise the Spirit also helps in our weaknesses.
For we do not know what we should pray for as we ought,
but the Spirit Himself makes intercession for us with
groanings which cannot be uttered.
Now He who searches the hearts
knows what the mind of the Spirit is,
because He makes intercession for the saints
according to the will of God.

ROMANS 8:26-27

The blessing of the LORD makes one rich,
and He adds no sorrow with it.

PROVERBS 10:22

Weeping may endure for a night,
but joy comes in the morning.

PSALM 30:5

Second Choice

~~~~~~

Choose to Express Your *Love* for God

8

Love Who He Is
Wholeheartedly

~~~~~~

The second major decision you must make—after the first major decision to *receive* God's love—is to *love God*. Consistently. Without doubt. With everything that is in you. No fingers crossed. No dipping your toes in the shallow end but instead plunging full force into the deepest part of the ocean of God's affection for you.

When you understand who God is and how much He loves you—and you open your heart to receive His love—then you cannot help but grow in love for Him. It just happens.

The amazing thing is that the more your love for Him grows, the more you will forget about who you *think* you are and begin to understand who He *made* you to be. God wants you to love Him so much that you walk closely enough with Him to allow the knowledge of who *He really is* define who *you really are*.

Expressing our love for God involves more than just feeling it. More than just saying a thank-you to Him when you think of it. Nothing is wrong with either of those things, but there are also specific decisions we need to make regarding how we live and relate to God.

The Bible not only tells us how much God loves us and how

far He has gone to assure us of His love, but it also tells us how we should express our love to *Him* in ways that please Him most.

Jesus instructed us to love Him with all of our being.

He said, "You shall love the LORD your God with *all your heart,* with *all your soul,* with *all your mind,* and with *all your strength*" (Mark 12:30).

That means wholeheartedly, with all that we have, by every means possible, with no holding back because our inner jury is still out on the verdict about Him.

Jesus instructed us to love Him more than anyone or anything.

He said, "He who loves father or mother more than Me is not worthy of Me. And he who loves son or daughter more than Me is not worthy of Me" (Matthew 10:37).

That doesn't mean we don't love our family members. It does mean we refuse to allow our love for anyone else to in any way diminish our love for God. In other words, we don't get so caught up with other people that we are too preoccupied to get caught up with *Him.* We seek His kingdom first, as He asks us to do, believing He will provide for those we love as well as for us because we are praying for them. This shows that we trust God to take care of them, knowing He loves them even more than we do.

Jesus instructed us to love Him more than wealth.

He said, "No one can serve two masters. Either you will hate the one and love the other, or you will be devoted to the one and despise the other. You cannot serve both God and money" (Matthew 6:24 NIV).

That means if we love money and possessions more than we love God, then we don't really love Him because we cannot do both. If our life is all about gaining wealth, then it's not all about serving God. If it's about loving riches, then it's not about being rich in the things of the Lord.

Wanting to make enough money to pay your bills doesn't mean you don't love God. But understanding where the money to pay the bills actually comes from means you recognize the source of everything you have. When you submit all you have to God and intend that your possessions glorify Him, then you are led by the love of God and not the love of money. *He* is directing you and not anyone or anything else.

Falling in Love with Someone Special

We have to know God intimately in order to love Him wholeheartedly. It requires great understanding and knowledge of who He is and what He thinks about you.

It takes falling in love with Him.

I was speaking at a large conference of women a week after Mother's Day, and I was talking about loving God. I asked the women to remember the way it was when they fell in love with someone. How it felt. Where they wanted to be. How they acted around the object of their affection.

I described it to them this way. See if it sounds accurate to you.

> When you fall in love, that special person you love occupies your every thought, so much so that it's hard to focus on anything else. You long for that person when you're not with them, and you cannot wait to be in their presence again. You are thrilled with everything you see about them. What's not to love, right? You want to know all there is to know about that person, so you often look lovingly at them for clues as to who they *are* and who they will *become*. You want to wrap your arms tightly around them and never let go. And every time you embrace that person, you feel new strength, fulfillment, joy, and life flowing into your being. You have deeply connected to that person at a depth you have always dreamed about, and your heart has found a home.

As I was describing all of this, I realized that each phrase perfectly described how I felt about the Mother's Day gift I had received just the week before. When my son and daughter-in-law handed me a small package wrapped in pink with a pink bow on top, I was smitten. She was 6 pounds, 13 ounces, and the moment I saw her it was love at first sight. My first grandchild—my granddaughter—was only minutes old, and yet she had a way of bringing such joy and happiness into my heart that I knew she was someone I would love forever.

What's not to love?

Every word I had said to the women at the conference to describe the way it feels to fall in love perfectly described the way I felt about my granddaughter. And I knew that because she was in my life I would never be the same again.

I told my son and daughter-in-law they should never even think of getting another Mother's Day present for me again. This one gift will perfectly cover every Mother's Day from now on. Unless, of course, they were thinking of giving me something similar in the future. When I said that, their eyes glazed over and they made the smallest attempt at a halfhearted smile. It had been too hard getting her here to think about that. They may reconsider in a few years, but even if they don't, I'm good forever with the way things are.

Feeling this kind of deep, committed love is a glorious way to feel. And that's the way God wants us to feel about *Him. All the time!*

Please read the above paragraph again that describes the way it feels to fall in love. Only this time, think of the words as how God wants *you* to feel about *Him.*

All the time!

Identifying Your Greatest Treasure

Jesus said, "*Where your treasure is, there your heart will be also*" (Matthew 6:21).

He isn't saying we can't have any earthly possessions or we can't enjoy what we have. He's saying we should not be selfishly motivated and materialistic regarding them. Our treasure should not be in what we own so that we are tied to that in a way that keeps us bound to what perishes, as opposed to building up eternal wealth in heaven. Our heart should not be with our possessions but instead with the One who is the source of all we have.

We must identify God in our heart as our greatest treasure.

Jesus spoke to a crowd of people about a wealthy fool who was rich in this life but did not lay up treasures in heaven. This man said to himself, "'What shall I do, since I have no room to store my crops?' So he said, 'I will do this: I will pull down my barns and build greater, and there I will store all my crops and my goods. And I will say to my soul, "Soul, you have many goods laid up for many years; take your ease; eat, drink, and be merry."' But God said to him, 'Fool! This night your soul will be required of you; then whose will those things be which you have provided?'" (Luke 12:17-20).

Jesus answered this question by saying, "So is he who lays up treasure for himself, and is not rich toward God" (Luke 12:21). He was speaking of people who were more concerned with possessions than with God. When they died, their possessions would be of no use to them, but those who used what they had to glorify God would have a reward in heaven for eternity.

Jesus talked to a rich young ruler who told Him he had kept all the commandments but now wondered what more he should do. Jesus answered, "If you want to be perfect, go, sell what you have and give to the poor, and you will have treasure in heaven; and come, follow Me" (Matthew 19:21). The rich ruler was saddened by that answer because he had great wealth and he wasn't about to give it up.

Although honestly acquired wealth is referred to in the Bible as part of God's blessing, how we handle it reveals our heart and attitude toward it. If we love God, our heart will not serve money but serve Him. That doesn't mean we can never have anything. It means we don't put our security in what we have. We put it in the Lord.

The important question: *Where is your greatest treasure?*
The answer to that: *It's where your heart is.*

We can't love God with our whole heart if our heart loves money, possessions, wealth, and riches more than it loves Him.

Ask God to show you where your heart is. The more you know of God, the more your heart will be with *Him*. And the evidence of your great love for Him will be that He is your greatest treasure.

We have to make room in our life for what matters most. When we find our greatest treasure and identify it as such, everything else pales in comparison.

Once I knew I was going to have a granddaughter, I took my daughter's old room (she is married now) and made it into a baby's room. When you love someone, you make room in your life for that special person. You do what it takes to please them and show them you value and care about them, and that they are not a burden. In fact, you find you have energy and time for your special person you didn't think you had before you realized who it is you truly love.

God wants you to make room in your life for *Him*. He wants you to express your love to Him in every way that pleases Him. He will give you energy and time you didn't know you could have. And not only that, He will help you show your love for Him in ways that not only please Him but will also be for your greatest blessing.

Prayer of *Love*

LORD, I love who You are and all You have done for me. I love all Your promises to me, and everything You have planned for my future. I am eternally grateful to be an heir of Your kingdom that You have given to those who love You (James 2:5). But even more than all of that, I simply want to love You with all my *heart, soul, mind,* and *strength* just as You desire (Mark 12:30). Help me to love You with my entire being, without compromise. Teach me how to accomplish that in every way that is pleasing to You.

I don't want to be like the Pharisees who tried to do everything perfectly—and legalistically—but bypassed the part about loving You (Luke 11:42). I know You see who has true love for You in their heart and who does not (John 5:42). I don't ever want You to see me offer You lukewarm or halfhearted love where You are concerned. I want to be able to show my adoration and consistently express my love for You in the most heartfelt ways.

Lord, Your Word says that if anyone loves You, that person is known by You (1 Corinthians 8:3). I want to be known by You in great depth, and to know You deeply as well. Help me to be "rooted and grounded in love" so that everything I do reflects my love for You (Ephesians 3:17). Thank You that You loved me long before I ever knew to love You (1 John 4:19). Now I love everything about You. Enable me to walk more closely to You every day so that I can know You more.

In Jesus' name I pray.

Words of *Love*

The LORD does not see as man sees;
for man looks at the outward appearance,
but the LORD looks at the heart.

1 SAMUEL 16:7

We have known and believed the love that God has for us.
God is love, and he who abides in love abides in God,
and God in him.

1 JOHN 4:16

Now hope does not disappoint, because the love of God
has been poured out in our hearts by the Holy Spirit
who was given to us.

ROMANS 5:5

We love Him because He first loved us.

1 JOHN 4:19

He who does not love does not know God,
for God is love.

1 JOHN 4:8

9

Live His Way
Uncompromisingly

~~~~~~

Time and again in the Old Testament, God's people—the Israelites—suffered because they did not love God enough to do what He told them to do. They lost sight of how to live His way. That's because they did not wholeheartedly love God, so they did not seek His presence. They refused to avoid the things that would compromise their relationship with Him, and they allowed themselves to become separate from Him.

The same is true for us today. We don't become separate from God unless we *choose* to be.

He never leaves *us*.

We leave *Him*.

We do that by living in disobedience to His ways. Our disregard for His laws puts up a barrier between us and Him until we can no longer hear Him speaking to our heart. And He won't listen to our prayers until we return to Him and take down the barrier. "The Lord's hand is not shortened, that it cannot save; nor His ear heavy, that it cannot hear. But *your iniquities have separated you from your God*; and *your sins have hidden His face from you*, so that *He will not hear*" (Isaiah 59:1-2).

It's not that He cannot hear; it's that He *will not* hear.

God does not refuse to listen to our prayers because He no longer loves us. It's because He *does* love us. If we want our prayers answered, we must get sin out of our lives and repent of it. That's the way it is.

Sin is demonic in its origin. The enemy comes to destroy us by leading us in opposition to God's ways. In fact, rebellion crouches at the door of our heart and waits for us to fall into deception so separation from God can creep in on us. It's subtle at first.

Sin often begins as a mere seed of a thought in the mind that is a lie from the enemy of our soul. It's designed to destroy us. As that thought is entertained by our desires, it grows until it guides our actions.

Too often we hear about a married Christian leader who has an affair outside of marriage. Surely that person chose their profession because they felt called by God and wanted to serve Him, so where did it all go wrong? At some point they allowed a thought into their mind that found a place to dwell in their heart until it became an action. And because of the distance all sin puts between a person and God, the still, small voice of the Holy Spirit to their heart could no longer be heard. Or if it was, there wasn't enough love for God in their heart to heed it, so it was ignored.

This can happen to anyone when they are blinded by pride to the point they think their needs are above God's laws. They don't love God above all else. Or they sort of love Him—but not enough.

The Bible says our sins testify *against us* until we confess them before God.

We separate *ourselves* from God because of our sins, and when we lie to ourselves about it, we are also lying to the Lord. We talk ourselves into believing a lie, such as "What I am doing is not that bad." "I deserve this." "This isn't hurting anyone." "No one will ever know." It all starts with a thought that is not born out of love for God and His ways and ends up with a heart that doesn't recognize who God really is.

The way to stop all this from happening is to love God and love His Word every bit as much.

Remember, Jesus is the living Word.

I have heard people say they can relate to Jesus but not to God. Or to God but not to the Holy Spirit. Whichever it is, that thinking is not right because God, Jesus, and the Holy Spirit are one. They are inseparable. We don't divide them up and choose sides. They are the three persons of the one true God. When we don't really get that, then we can't receive the fullness of *God's love* for us because we don't understand all that God is and all that He does. Nor can we fully show *our love* for God.

Because of my past I was not taught much about the Word of God. In fact, I never heard that term until I was an adult. And I didn't receive much instruction about life, either. So I had to learn many things the hard way.

I observed good, godly traits and habits in my dad. For example, he was kind and not mean in stark contrast to my mother. He worked hard to support the family in spite of one hardship after another. In one year alone a record blizzard killed his cattle in the winter and a record hailstorm destroyed his crops in the spring, and we were forced to leave our home, but I never heard him complain. He never used foul language. He was not a raging alcoholic or drug user. He was not a womanizer, nor did he ever stray from his home. He taught me good things by his example.

My mother, on the other hand, was irrational and unpredictably violent. During her crazy episodes she used language so foul I have never heard anything as bad to this day. Usually it was directed at me. Today I understand that this was part of her mental illnesses, but not back then. I just thought it was somehow my fault—that my existence provoked her to such extremes. And maybe it did.

We never went to church as a family that I remember. My father avoided it in the same way one would avoid a highly contagious and deadly disease. He told me that once he left his parents' home he vowed he would never enter another church as long as he lived. As far as I know he didn't.

There was a large Bible in our house that, to my knowledge, had not been opened for years. When I was about fourteen, we moved to another town and my mother tried harder to be normal. It was as though she was attempting to make a new start. She and I attended a little Episcopal church where we even sang in the choir. I saw her open up that Bible a few times and read it, although I was never tempted to do that myself. It bordered on a semi-positive experience until the day she stormed into the living room, opened up the back door, and threw the Bible out in the dirt in the backyard. And that was the end of the Bible and the church. She could only keep it together for so long before she became mad at God. Then she descended back into her dark and violent world. Sadly, she never knew the love and power of God that can heal and transform. That's what happens when the Holy Spirit is totally left out of the equation and God is misunderstood.

Aside from that brief experience, I never actually learned what the Bible said. Had I been instructed specifically in the ways of God, I could have avoided the horrible mistakes I made. Although much can be learned by both observation and experience, having even the most basic foundation in God's Word would have made all the difference in my being able to avoid the foolish and dangerous things I did.

There are so many important things we will never learn anywhere else except from God's Word. That's because every time we read or hear God's Word with an open heart and spiritually opened eyes, a transformative dynamic happens in the process.

The truth is, we become slaves to whomever we obey. We can either become a slave to our own sin or a slave to the Lord and His ways. If we don't know the Lord's ways, what is the end result?

Some people mistakenly believe they are "free" and therefore not restricted by God's rules and laws, but they are actually enslaved by their own greed, lust, obsessions, indulgence, self-focus, bitterness, unforgiveness, bad habits, apathy, anger, or whatever else is not God's will for them. The Bible says we *were slaves of sin,*" but when we received the Lord we were set free to become "*slaves of righteousness*" (Romans 6:17-18).

Our love for God—and expression of that love to Him—establishes our foundation in Christ and allows us to become slaves to His righteousness.

That is *true freedom.*

Show Love for God by Living His Way

Reading the Bible is like looking into the magnifying mirror I described in the first chapter. That is exactly the way an in-depth reading of God's Word exposes the imperfections in us. The more we seek God in His Word, the more He shows us where we need to become more like *Him.* Every time we look into His Word, He not only reveals more of who *He is,* but He also shows us more of who *we are.* He then grows us to reflect His nature and character.

If we live according to His Word, we gain His favor because of our obedience. "*The LORD rewarded me according to my righteousness; according to the cleanness of my hands He has recompensed me. For I have kept the ways of the LORD, and have not wickedly departed from my God*" (Psalm 18:20-21).

Jesus made it clear that living His way demonstrates our love for Him.

He said, "*He who has My commandments and keeps them, it is he who loves Me. And he who loves Me will be loved by My Father, and I will love him and manifest Myself to him…If anyone loves Me, he will keep My word; and My Father will love him, and We will come to him and make Our home with him*" (John 14:21,23).

There is a clear connection between our obedience to God's Word and God's presence in our lives. God the Father, Son, and Holy Spirit will make their home with us when we show our love for God by keeping His commandments.

It can't get any clearer than that.

We read the Bible not just for information but for revelation from God. Every time we read His Word we can sense His presence. And when we become familiar with God's voice speaking to us from His Word, we will then be able to recognize His voice speaking to our heart when we are *not* reading his Word at that moment.

John, the brother of Jesus, said, "*This is the love of God, that we keep His commandments.* And His commandments are not burdensome" (1 John 5:3).

His commandments are not too hard because He helps us to do them when we ask Him to.

Show Love for God by Asking Him to Help You *Do* His Word

Another great thing God does for us is that He not only gives us His guide to a *good* life—His commandments, rules, precepts, and laws—but He also *helps* us to obey them.

God enables us to live His way when we ask Him to do so.

He knows our weaknesses and that we end up doing things we don't want to do because of them. But when we make it our *desire* and *delight* to do His Word, it pleases Him because it demonstrates our love for Him.

"*Be doers of the word, and not hearers only,* deceiving yourselves. For *if anyone is a hearer of the word and not a doer, he is like a man observing his natural face in a mirror,* for he observes himself, goes away, and immediately forgets what kind of man he was" (James 1:22-24).

There is that mirror illustration again.

If we only hear the Word and don't *do* it, we not only cannot see our true selves reflected clearly, we don't really understand who God made us to be. But if we look "*into the perfect law of liberty*" and are "*not a forgetful hearer but a doer of the work*" we will be blessed in all we do (James 1:25).

That means we can forget who we are when we just hear or read God's laws. It's in the *doing* of them that our knowledge of God's Word takes root and we come to understand who He created us to be.

God's laws ignite our conscience. We have a battle going on between our new nature and our old nature (Romans 7:19-25). Our flesh wants to do what it wants even though our mind wants to obey God.

Jesus questioned why people called Him "Lord" and didn't do what He asked them to do (Luke 6:46). We obviously don't have the right to call Him Lord if we are not living *His* way. Our rebellion against His laws means He doesn't really have the place of prominence in our heart and life.

We show love for God by refusing to live in disobedience to Him and also by recognizing we *can't* live His way without Him *helping* us to do so.

Paul warns that we can't resist lust and idolatry without the power of God giving us strength. When we ask Him, He will enable us to do the right thing. Paul said, "*Let him who thinks he stands take heed lest he fall.* No temptation has overtaken you except such as is common to man; but God is faithful, who will not allow you to be tempted beyond what you are able, but *with the temptation will also make the way of escape*, that you may be able to bear it" (1 Corinthians 10:12-13).

We can choose to obey, but it is the power of the Holy Spirit in us that enables us to do it. With His power working in us, we can resist anything.

Show Love for God by Refusing to Create Your Own Suffering

I have often cited King David's life examples in this book because he was a real and fallible human being who had a loving heart toward God and wanted to do right, but he fell into temptation to not live God's way and experienced needless suffering because of it. There are other people in the Bible like that as well, but they didn't write about their feelings and experiences in clear, deep, and relatable ways as much as David did. When he repented of what he had done, it was deeply heartfelt—often gut wrenchingly so—and God forgave him.

He was a lot like we are. We bring needless suffering upon ourselves too.

While we may have never done anything as bad as David, we certainly have had need for repentance in our lives.

David recognized that his suffering was because of his own disobedience and he was drowning in the consequences. "*My iniquities have gone over my head; like a heavy burden they are too heavy for me. My wounds are foul and festering because of my foolishness. I am troubled*, I am bowed down greatly; *I go mourning* all the day long" (Psalm 38:4-6). "*My iniquities have overtaken me*, so that I am not able to look up; they are more than the hairs of my head; *therefore my heart fails me*" (Psalm 40:12).

A burden too heavy to bear, festering wounds, sorrow, guilt, mourning, and heart failure, all because of unconfessed sin? It's not worth it. Let's repent as soon as possible. Let's ask God to etch His law in our heart like a tattoo so we don't ever leave home without it.

David often thought God didn't see or hear him anymore because of his failure to live God's way. But God *did* hear David's prayers because of his repentant heart. "I said in my haste, 'I am cut off from before Your eyes'; nevertheless You heard the voice of my supplications when I cried out to You" (Psalm 31:22).

God loves us enough to allow us to go through the fire when He wants to purify us. He allows us to go through floodwaters, which cleanse us. He lets us suffer when it will mold our heart for His kingdom. "You, O God, have tested us; You have refined us as silver is refined…*we went through fire and through water; but You brought us out to rich fulfillment*" (Psalm 66:10,12).

How many times have we, too, said, "God doesn't hear my prayers. He doesn't see my need"? The truth is that He *does* hear and He *does* see, but sometimes we have unconfessed and unrepented sin, such as doubt, unforgiveness, unresolved anger, lying…the list is endless. We have to ask Him to show us.

Sometimes it's not a sin problem. It's just that God wants us to wait on Him in faith for the answers to our prayers. So we must ask Him in those times if He is perhaps waiting on *us* for something. Waiting on us to obey Him? Waiting on us to hear His leading? Waiting on us to lay down our idols? Or is He testing our faith and obedience?

David asked who could dwell with God and then answered his own question by saying, "He who *walks uprightly*, and *works righteousness*, and *speaks the truth in his heart*" (Psalm 15:2). Ask God if you are always speaking truth in your heart. The way to keep your heart from becoming deceitful is to wash it daily in the Word.

Scripture says that God guides us with His eye (Psalm 32:8). If He is to guide us with His eye, that means we have to be looking to Him.

That means we have to be looking into His Word as well.

Show Love for God by Asking Him to Reveal What Is in Your Heart

Because we cannot always see our own sins, we need to ask God to reveal them to us. "*Who can understand his errors? Cleanse me from secret faults*" (Psalm 19:12). God hates sin and we don't want something in our lives that God hates. Getting rid of sin is one of the most important ways we show our love for Him. That's the way we keep from doing something we are tempted to do.

We love God too much to allow it to happen.

We show love for God by asking him to show us anything in our heart that should not be there. David said, "*Search me, O God, and know my heart;* try me, and know my anxieties; *and see if there is any wicked way in me*, and lead me in the way everlasting" (Psalm 139:23-24).

God showed David what was in his heart just as he asked. The trouble was that too often David should have asked much sooner than he did. He should have asked the night he was up on his roof watching the woman next door take a bath. Actually, he shouldn't have been there that night in the first place. He was supposed to be out on the battlefield with his soldiers at war.

When God revealed what was in David's heart, he repented and God forgave him. But he should have done so sooner.

We can also ask God to reveal what is in our heart as we read His Word. And we can ask Him to help us be free of whatever is not of Him.

Jesus said, "If you abide in My word, you are My disciples indeed. And *you shall know the truth, and the truth shall make you free*" (John 8:31-32).

This doesn't mean we are set free by just *any* truth. We can know the truth about a lot of things and never get free of anything. Only knowing *God's* truth truly sets us free.

In order to be set free by God's truth, His Word must be planted in our heart. God's Word says to "*receive with meekness the implanted word*, which is able to save your souls" (James 1:21). If we water, nourish, and cherish the implanted Word, it will grow into great strength, wisdom, courage, and a sense of what's right.

Jesus also said, "*If you keep My commandments, you will abide in My love*, just as I have kept My Father's commandments and abide in His love. These things I have spoken to you, that My joy may remain in you, and that your joy may be full" (John 15:10-11).

Jesus proved His love for us by going to the cross to pay the consequences for our sins. "Greater love has no one than this, than to lay down one's life for his friends" (John 15:13). We need to prove our love for Him by going to the foot of the cross and asking Him to expose our heart and set us free of anything that keeps us from living in the fullness of His joy.

No greater love, indeed.

Show Love for God by Letting His Word Change You

When you love God's Word, it changes you every time you read it. You can be anxious about something, but when you read the

Scriptures, you will feel God's love taking away your fears. The more you sense God's love, the more your love for Him grows, and the more that changes you.

Make time every day to be changed by God's Word. Ask Him to speak to you as you read it. Tell Him you choose to live His way and not in opposition to it. Refuse to be a part of anything that is questionable. You will find yourself growing in the Lord to the same degree that you grow in His Word. Without having your roots in *His truth*, you will not mature in truth. You will just be learning facts. There is nothing wrong with that, but in order to be changed you have to receive more. You can have knowledge of the Word and not be touched or changed by it. You want to be *transformed* and *not* just *informed*.

The Bible says we shall bear fruit and flourish into old age so we can declare that the Lord is good and He is our foundation on which we stand. "Those who are planted in the house of the LORD shall flourish in the courts of our God. *They shall still bear fruit in old age; they shall be fresh and flourishing*" (Psalm 92:13-14).

The only way we bear fruit into old age is if seeds from God's Word are planted in our heart now so they can grow into something big. Ask God to remove anything from your heart that would not allow those seeds to grow. Tell God every day, "I will delight myself in Your commandments, which I love" (Psalm 119:47).

Then act accordingly.

Prayer of *Love*

LORD, I pray You would help me to live Your way without compromise. Teach me Your laws and commands so they are etched upon my heart. "Your word is a lamp to my feet and a light to my path" (Psalm 119:105). Guide me every day in the way I should go. Your laws are good and more desirable than fine gold, and You have a great reward for those who keep them (Psalm 19:9-11). Thank You that because I love Your ways, You have anointed me "with the oil of gladness" (Psalm 45:7).

I love Your laws because I know they are right and they keep me from stumbling, and all who keep them have great peace (Psalm 119:165). I know that "all Your commandments are truth" and they have been true and unfailing forever (Psalm 119:151). "I rejoice at Your word as one who finds great treasure" (Psalm 119:162). Help me to always feel that way. Make my faith to grow as I read and hear Your Word (Romans 10:17).

I love Your ways and despise "*the ways of those who don't*...Rivers of water run down from my eyes, because men do not keep Your law" (Psalm 119:128,136). It grieves me to see people disregard Your laws. I know it grieves You even more when I do the same. You see my "secret sins" (Psalm 90:8), so I ask You to expose them if I am allowing something into my mind and heart that should not be there. I will confess it before You so that I can be forgiven and remove any separation between You and me. "You are my hiding place and my shield; I hope in Your word" (Psalm 119:114).

In Jesus' name I pray.

Words of *Love*

Great peace have those who love Your law,
and nothing causes them to stumble.

PSALM 119:165

Do not forget my law,
but let your heart keep my commands;
for length of days and long life
and peace they will add to you.

PROVERBS 3:1-2

I have restrained my feet from every evil way,
that I may keep Your word.

PSALM 119:101

Give me understanding,
that I may learn Your commandments.
Those who fear You will be glad when they see me,
because I have hoped in Your word.

PSALM 119:73-74

Unless Your law had been my delight,
I would then have perished in my affliction.
I will never forget Your precepts, for by them You have
given me life.

PSALM 119:92-93

10

Learn to
Worship Him Lavishly

One of the most powerful ways to express our love for God is by worshipping Him. It's the purest form of adoration because we are focused completely on Him and not on ourselves.

The Bible says, "Let everything that has breath praise the LORD" (Psalm 150:6). As long as we are still breathing on this earth, we should "praise Him for His mighty acts" and "according to His excellent greatness" (Psalm 150:2). In other words, praise Him *for what He has done* and *for who He is.*

God is not asking us to worship Him because He has an ego that needs to be stroked. It's because He wants us to honor Him with the reverence that is due Him. Plus, in the expressing of our love, adoration, and reverence for Him, He opens up a channel through which we connect with Him and become the closest to Him we can ever be on this earth.

Showing Love for God in Worship Changes You

We all worship something whether we realize it or not. Some people worship money, possessions, themselves, their animals, or their political party. Others make idols out of their work, their children, their talent, their friends, the sun, the moon, the ocean, a sport, an occupation, nature, beauty, music, celebrities, hobbies, or entertainment. The list is endless. Whatever it is, it's an attempt to fulfill the human need to worship something or someone.

Whatever we worship will be the biggest motivator of all we do and have the greatest influence on our lives.

The truth is, there is only One who is worthy of our worship, and if we don't understand that, we will miss out on great blessings we can never receive any other way.

We were born to worship God. It's the way He shares Himself with us. As we worship Him, He pours Himself into us—His love, power, joy, peace, and wisdom—and in the process He transforms us into who we were created to be. We become like what we worship, so the more we worship God, the more we become like Him (Psalm 115:4-8). And we cannot become all we were created to be without that happening.

One of the most amazing things about God is that even though our worship and praise are directed solely at Him, we are the ones who benefit. Isn't it just like our loving God to make something that is totally about Him to be the key to our greatest blessing?

Expressing our love for God in worship and praise fulfills us in ways we didn't realize we could be filled—in ways we didn't even know we were empty. That's because He wants to give us certain blessings that can only happen when we are praising Him. Every time we worship Him, something changes in us—in our mind, emotions, attitudes, desires, or goals.

The more you understand who God is, the more you will love Him. The closer you walk with Him, the more you will worship Him and be changed by Him.

Praise God No Matter What Is Happening in Your Life

God's kingdom is invited into our lives in a powerful way every time we lift up praise and worship to Him. Our worship demonstrates our love for Him and opens the way for Him to work powerfully in our lives to transform us and our impossible situations. That's why it's God's will that we give thanks and praise to Him *in every situation*. When we don't do that, we shut off possibilities for great things God wants to do in our life. Worship can even stop or reverse something that is headed in the wrong direction.

There have been countless times in my life as a believer where I prayed and prayed about a problem, praising God that He cared about a particular situation and He was greater than what I was facing. But there came a time when God instructed my heart that I was to continue praising Him no matter what did or did not happen. I was to trust that He had the answer to what was needed and the power to change things, and His timing and judgment were perfect. I took that stance of trust in Him until breakthrough finally came.

Worship establishes an atmosphere in which God moves powerfully. Things happened that I believe would not have without that powerful dynamic.

God requires worship and praise of all of who believe in Him because He wants us to be sold out to Him one hundred percent. And He does that because He has so much He wants to give us and do in our lives, and He must be able to trust us with the blessings we will receive.

"*Let the peoples praise You*, O God; let all the peoples praise You. *Then the earth shall yield her increase; God, our own God, shall bless us.* God shall bless us, and all the ends of the earth shall fear Him" (Psalm 67:5-7). Blessings happen to people who worship Him.

What parent doesn't want their children to express love and appreciation for them without wanting something? God wants that too. That's why we need to make worship of Him a priority, not just something we may or may not remember to do. It must become a way of life.

We were created to worship God, and when we are doing what we were *created* to do, we more quickly move into other aspects of our purpose as well.

On the day that God delivered David from his enemies, he worshipped God *before* the victory happened, saying, "The Lord is *my rock* and *my fortress* and *my deliverer*; my God, *my strength*, in whom I will trust; *my shield* and the horn of my salvation, *my stronghold*. I will call upon the Lord, who is worthy to be praised; so shall I be saved from my enemies" (Psalm 18:2-3).

David didn't wait for the victory, or the answer to prayer, or for everything to turn out right. He worshipped God until the victory happened. We need to do the same.

God wants us to worship Him lavishly. "Lavishly" means to go all out, hold nothing back, offer freely with both hands, spare no expense, and give generously without counting the cost.

When you worship God in that way, telling Him of your love, adoration, affection, devotion, passion, respect, awe, and reverence of Him, great changes are certain to be in you and your life.

When you exalt, cherish, hold dear, revere, and glorify the Lord for all He has done, you will be filled with His love, joy, peace, and power as well as compassion and love for others. All of those things will be infused into you like a life-giving serum. It will determine who you become. It doesn't determine who God made you to be, but who God made you to be will be more fully realized in a way that will not happen without a heart of lavish worship for Him.

Worship will always be your greatest act of love toward God. And it will be because of a *choice* you make. If you choose not to praise and worship God until everything is going the way you want it to or until your prayers have been answered, you will miss what God wants to do in your life.

Worship Him at *all times* because He is always—every moment of the day—worthy of it. Let His praise continually be in your heart and your mouth. Soon you will not be able to stop yourself from worshipping Him.

There Is Never a Time When You Don't Need to Worship God

Those who do not worship God soon forget all He has done.

When the Israelites didn't worship God, they started worshipping their own ways. They stopped seeking His counsel. And they did that even after God had done many obvious miracles in order to free them. They complained and lusted after other things and were not thankful for what He had provided for them. So God let them have what they wanted, but there was an enormous price to pay.

"*They soon forgot His works*; they *did not wait for His counsel*, but lusted exceedingly in the wilderness, and tested God in the desert. *And He gave them their request, but sent leanness into their soul*" (Psalm 106:13-15).

A lean and empty soul will never be satisfied or filled. There will never be enough. It will always be miserable.

Every time we worship God with all of our heart, He fills our emptiness with Himself. "Oh, that men would give thanks to the LORD for His goodness, and for His wonderful works to the children of men! *For He satisfies the longing soul, and fills the hungry soul with goodness*" (Psalm 107:8-9).

We can't ever allow ourselves to get into the situation where we believe we don't need to worship God. We must not think for a moment that nothing can shake us—that we don't need God and we can't fail. We must not have a false sense of security and suppose we don't need to pour ourselves out before the Lord in praise and empty ourselves before Him in humble worship. We cannot imagine for even an instant that God's rules don't apply to us.

That's what David did the day he ordered his troops to be counted. He listened to the enemy's lies instead of showing love, adoration, and thanksgiving to God in worship. "Satan stood up against Israel, and moved David to number Israel" (1 Chronicles 21:1). So David told his leader, Joab, to number the troops. But Joab had the fear of God in him and tried to talk David out of doing that because he knew it would displease the Lord.

Joab pleaded, "Why then does my lord require this thing? Why should he be a cause of guilt in Israel?" (1 Chronicles 21:3). But David would not be dissuaded and the troops were counted.

David's thinking was that the number of his soldiers was what gave him strength and security. He forgot it was *God* who was *with them* that brought him victory.

When David finally recognized his sin against God, his "heart condemned him" and He mourned because of it (2 Samuel 24:10). He confessed and repented of it before God, but he still had to pay the consequences, which was a plague that killed seventy thousand men (2 Samuel 24:15).

All this happened because he didn't humbly worship God, which would have softened his heart to hear God's voice, and then he would not have listened to the voice of the enemy.

David had been the great lavish worshipper, the one who went all out and gave himself totally to worshipping God, but pride crept into his heart. As a result he suffered a reduction in the number of troops he had, the very thing he was most proud of. He paid an enormous price—but so did his men, I might add. This only goes to show why the Bible says we are to pray for all people who are in authority over us (1 Timothy 2:2).

David was fully restored to God because of his repentant heart. He said to God, "You have turned for me my mourning into dancing; You have put off my sackcloth and clothed me with gladness, *to the end that my glory may sing praise to You and not be silent.* O LORD my God, I will give thanks to You forever" (Psalm 30:11-12).

David recognized that when things were going well he thought he could not be shaken. He said, "In my prosperity I said, 'I shall never be moved'" (Psalm 30:6). This is the mistake too many of us make when we fail to see where our help comes from and why we should look to the Lord at all times (Psalm 121:1-2).

We have to ask ourselves if there is anything we are counting on to save us more than we are relying on God. Are we adding up things in order to fortify ourselves instead of adding up what God *has done, is doing,* and *can do* in our lives and thanking Him for that? There is never a time when we don't need to worship God. If we think there is, then we are listening to the wrong voice.

God Blesses Those Who Worship Him Together

Something powerful happens when we worship God with other people. This doesn't diminish the worship that happens in our heart between us and God alone, but we receive another powerful blessing when we worship corporately with other believers in unity of spirit and mind. And that blessing doesn't happen any other way.

Much is said in the Bible about the importance of worshipping with other believers. *"Let them exalt Him also in the assembly of the people"* (Psalm 107:32). *"My praise shall be of You in the great assembly;* I will pay my vows before those who fear Him" (Psalm 22:25).

David told God that he did not want to be in "the assembly of evildoers," but he wanted to be in the house of the Lord to "proclaim with the voice of thanksgiving, and tell of all Your wondrous works. LORD, *I have loved the habitation of Your house, and the place where Your glory dwells"* (Psalm 26:5,7-8). "My foot stands in an even place; *in the congregations I will bless the LORD"* (Psalm 26:12).

When we are in the house of the Lord proclaiming praise and worship to Him, we are in His presence and our feet are on solid ground. Loving the house of God doesn't mean we love a building, but that we love where God's presence is invited to dwell and is exalted among the people with their praise and worship. God's presence dwells where He is worshipped and invited. In God's house we can sense the awesome power of His presence in response to our worship. It affects us with strength, rejuvenation, a sense of clarity, and purpose. We are able to better hear from God. There is great breakthrough that may not happen otherwise.

Praising Him corporately by lifting up our hands to Him in worship is an act of surrender and humility (Psalm 134:2). It's like saying

"We give up." But we are not giving up on God. We are giving up trying to do things without Him. We are surrendering to Him.

When We Praise God, His Presence Dwells with Us

Our praise is the most immediate and certain way to experience God's presence. Even though God is everywhere, certain degrees and manifestations of His presence are only experienced by those who express their love for Him through praise and worship.

God dwells in the praises of His people. The Bible says, "*You are holy, enthroned in the praises of Israel*" (Psalm 22:3). But God doesn't just visit for the moments we are worshipping Him and then He is gone. He *stays dwelling with us*. Jesus said, "*God is Spirit, and those who worship Him must worship in spirit and truth*" (John 4:24). When we express our love for God with our worship, we humbly recognize the truth of who He is and who we are in relation to Him, and we open up to a powerful fresh infusion of the presence of His Spirit that stays with us.

Our reverence for God demonstrates humility. A humble heart of worship and praise is beautiful to Him. "Rejoice in the LORD, O you righteous! For praise from the upright is beautiful" (Psalm 33:1). The beauty of the Lord beautifies us when we worship Him. "The LORD takes pleasure in His people; He will beautify the humble with salvation" (Psalm 149:4).

Worship beautifies us because as we look to God, His beauty reflects in us.

When you want to be closer to God, then "enter into His gates with thanksgiving, and into His courts with praise" and "be thankful to Him, and bless His name" (Psalm 100:4). When you praise God, He will manifest His power and love to you. His power and love do not fade, nor does His presence, but we cannot tap into it as fully when we don't have praise and worship of Him in our heart. That's why we don't just praise Him once and we're done. We do *not* summon His presence like a genie. We praise Him continually.

When we praise Him lavishly, He lavishly gifts us with His presence.

Prayer of *Love*

LORD, I worship You for who You are and I praise You for all You have done in my life. Teach me how to worship You lavishly with all that is in me. Help me to glorify Your name in worship always (Psalm 86:12). Your name alone is exalted, and Your glory is "above the earth and heaven" (Psalm 148:13). Let Your high praise always be in my mouth and a two-edged sword in my hand (Psalm 149:6).

Help me to never number my assets as David did to give glory to anyone or anything other than You as the source of all my blessings. Show me any place in my life where I am doing that. I don't want leanness to creep into my soul. I only want the fullness of life and heart that You have for me. Thank You that You satisfy my hungry soul with Your goodness (Psalm 107:8-9). Thank You that "in the day when I cried out, You answered me, and made me bold with strength in my soul" (Psalm 138:3).

I come before You with thanksgiving and worship only You. "You are my God, and I will praise You" and exalt You above all else (Psalm 118:28). I give You all the glory due You because You are worthy of praise. I worship You in the beauty of Your holiness (Psalm 29:2). I proclaim that this is the day You have made and I will rejoice and be glad in it (Psalm 118:24). "Be exalted, O God, above the heavens; let Your glory be above all the earth" (Psalm 57:11).

In Jesus' name I pray.

Words of *Love*

Bless the LORD, O my soul;
and all that is within me, bless His holy name!

PSALM 103:1

Because Your lovingkindness is better than life,
my lips shall praise You.
Thus I will bless You while I live;
I will lift up my hands in Your name.

PSALM 63:3-4

The hour is coming, and now is, when the true worshipers
will worship the Father in spirit and truth;
for the Father is seeking such to worship Him.

JOHN 4:23

I will sing to the LORD as long as I live;
I will sing praise to my God while I have my being.
May my meditation be sweet to Him;
I will be glad in the LORD.

PSALM 104:33-34

It is good to give thanks to the LORD,
and to sing praises to Your name, O Most High;
to declare Your lovingkindness in the morning,
and Your faithfulness every night.

PSALM 92:1-2

11

Look for Ways to Trust Him Completely

~~~~~~

L ove and trust go hand in hand.

We show our love for God every time we deliberately put our trust in Him. The reason we won't be disappointed in doing that is *"because the love of God has been poured out in our hearts by the Holy Spirit who was given to us"* (Romans 5:5).

God's love poured into us by the indwelling Holy Spirit is unfailing. That's because *He* is unfailing. His love is not a sometimes-maybe-possibly-perhaps-might-happen-comes-and-goes kind of thing. The Holy Spirit poured out in our heart is constant.

Because God shares Himself with us, we can certainly trust Him. Looking for ways to trust God completely doesn't mean we have to search hard to find anything in our lives that requires faith on our part. Everything we do of any worth requires trust in God. Too often we are tempted to give up—or give in—just when we should decide we are going to give God our complete trust.

You are going to have times in your life when you have to trust God in the situation you are in. You cannot do anything to change it, but you can worry yourself sick over it, and that still won't change anything—except that you'll be sick. You must trust that God is the only source of miracle-working power you need.

My daughter-in-law, Paige, had Ewing's Sarcoma, a serious bone cancer, when she was eleven years old. She was in the hospital for nearly a year receiving chemotherapy and having multiple surgeries to replace her damaged leg and knee bones. Because so many children her age died of this terrible disease, including kids she knew in the hospital, it was a miracle she survived. And there were no reliable statistics on what the chances were she would ever be able to have children. There were no guarantees from any doctor about this.

After she and our son were married, we all prayed and prayed that she would be able to become pregnant, and in two years in a story that is only hers to tell, she did. After she was expecting, we started worrying whether everything would turn out well for her and the baby. That kind of worry was beyond what we could handle, and so in prayer we came to the conclusion that Paige's recovery and life were already miracles, her pregnancy was a miracle, and God doesn't do partial miracles. He does complete miracles. No matter what we feared, we were going to keep praying and trusting Him all the way through the delivery that Paige and baby would be perfectly healthy and have no complications. And that is exactly what happened. Mother and daughter came through with no problems, and we had peace throughout the process.

We all have opportunities like this where we can make a decision *to trust God* completely in a potentially worrisome situation, but we must also ask Him to show us how to approach each concern in prayer. In other words, we don't walk out into the middle of oncoming traffic or jump off a building trusting that He will protect us. Jesus Himself didn't do that. We don't dictate the outcome to God. We ask Him how we are to pray and then trust Him to answer in His way and time.

There are many ways to decide you are going to trust God in the situation at hand. Below are just a few of them.

Trust God to Deliver You from Danger

God gives us a secret place to dwell that keeps us hidden from danger. *"He who dwells in the secret place of the Most High shall abide under the shadow of the Almighty. I will say of the LORD, 'He is my refuge and my fortress; my God, in Him I will trust'"*(Psalm 91:1-2). We can hide ourselves in the Lord and trust Him to protect us.

The key here is dwelling every day with the Lord and staying under the umbrella of His protection by living His way. It pleases Him when we diligently obey Him and deliberately trust Him to protect us.

Even in difficult times, God will preserve you because you make Him your dwelling place.

Can you think of times in your life when angels must have stepped in to protect you? I remember many times like that. One such time was during the first winter after we moved from California to Tennessee. Back then I thought "ice storm" was a metaphor for an especially cold rain. One day I was venturing out for needed groceries. I had not yet learned that when the weatherman predicts an ice storm, you get groceries beforehand for seven to ten days. Four days after the storm things looked melted enough to me, so I ventured forth. As I was driving I did not see a large patch of black ice. I had never even heard of "black ice" before that day, or if I had I probably thought it was some kind of frozen Halloween party drink. I was from California, after all.

As I drove slowly down a small incline, I intended to stop at the intersection where I had the red light. But much to my shock, and certainly the shock of all the other drivers around, instead of stopping I slid right into the intersection and spun out in the busy traffic that was moving in both directions on the cross street in front of me. I had never experienced the sensation of being completely out of control in a car before. Any number of cars could have hit me, but one particular car headed right toward me. That person obviously could not stop either because black ice covered the intersection. I braced for impact and prayed, "Jesus, help me"—the shortest prayer I knew—and the other driver and I totally missed each other.

I'm sure that driver was as surprised as I was that we didn't crash. It was truly as if an angel stuck out his hand and kept us apart like an invisible air bag. I could feel the air between us—or lack thereof— that jostled our cars. There was no other explanation for it.

In the Bible, it sounds as though we must have at least two angels who are assigned to protect us because the word for "angel" is plural. It says of God that *"He shall give His angels charge over you, to keep you in all your ways. In their hands they shall bear you up, lest you dash your foot against a stone"* (Psalm 91:11-12). Jesus often referred to multiple angels when He was on earth. I figure that between me and the other driver, we had at least four angels. I don't know if the other driver was a believer in the Lord or had been a praying person, but I would think he would have become one in that moment. My concept of "fervent prayer" was clarified in that moment as well.

The point is, God knows how to protect us from danger and can do so when we make Him our refuge.

Trust God to Take Away Your Fear

The Bible says you don't have to live in fear. Not living in fear doesn't mean being stupidly fearless. There are things you should be afraid of, but you don't have to be controlled by fear or make it a way of life.

For example, you *should* be afraid to leave the door to your house open all night because of what could happen to you and your family. But you could also trust God that if you accidentally left the door open, He would answer your ongoing prayers for protection and give you grace for that mistake.

The Bible says, "You shall not be afraid of the *terror* by night, nor of the *arrow* that flies by day, nor of the *pestilence* that walks in darkness, nor of the *destruction* that lays waste at noonday" (Psalm 91:5- 6). But how do we not be afraid when those kinds of threats are all around us? The threats of terrorizing acts, of crazy people using weapons against others, of diseases and plagues, and of destructive forces of nature—they are always on our mind. How do we handle those possible threats to our safety?

David trusted God to hear his prayers and give him relief for his troubled mind, soul, and body. He said to God, "*The troubles of my heart have enlarged; bring me out of my distresses!*" (Psalm 25:17). Can it be that some of our heart problems, and the conditions that bring them on, have a lot to do with the way we handle stress in our lives? Stress is a form of fear.

My husband and I had a tiny, long-haired Chihuahua named Sammy who did not handle stress well. Thunder was the most traumatic thing in his life, and at the mere flash of lightning, even before the thunder sounded, he would shake so violently I thought his shaking alone might make his heart stop.

Yet if someone left the gate open in the backyard, he would run out and down the driveway, across the street, and travel block after block, exploring this fascinating world and never looking back. Thank God that in His mercy we or a nice neighbor were always able to get ahold of him before disaster happened.

Sammy was afraid of something he didn't need to be afraid of but fearless concerning something that was extremely dangerous. He was never in any danger from the storm, even though he remained unconvinced of that. But he would leave the safety of his yard in a heartbeat, even though there were animals out in the world that would eat him for lunch and people in big cars who would not even see him before they ran over him, not to mention unethical people who might steal him.

Sammy developed a heart condition that many of these types of dogs have in later years. His heart kept enlarging until he was about twelve years old. By that time his heart was so big it was pressing against his esophagus, causing him to choke. We gave him special supplements and medicines from the veterinarian, but we could only slow down the progress of his enlarging heart. We could not stop it.

Every thunderstorm brought more and more terror to him, even though there was no way we would ever allow him to be hurt by it. I held him through many storms, but he could not be consoled. The noise was overwhelmingly frightening for him, and he never stopped shaking violently. The doctor gave us medicine to calm him, but he became too weak to take it.

One night I tried to hold him through a thunderstorm, but it went on for hours and he was so sick I knew that to give him a tranquilizer would surely kill him. I had to be up early and trying to calm him did nothing, so I let him stay in our large closet where he liked to go during storms because there are no windows and he couldn't see the lightning or hear the thunder as well. The closet was connected to the bathroom, where I left his bowl of water because he panted so hard and long that I knew he would be thirsty once the thunder stopped.

When my husband and I woke up in the morning, we found that Sammy had died in his sleep during the night in the same position he always liked to curl up in during storms—in the farthest corner where he could get away from the door and hide under some clothes that hung down to the floor. We were so sad that we cried for months over his loss. He had been a loving and faithful friend and family member, and quite a threatening chief of our security detail.

I wonder how many of us shorten our lives a little every day, like Sammy, as we run headlong into what we need to fear most but are terrified to the point of incapacitation over what we don't need to fear at all. We take on stress in our lives that we don't need instead of taking our stress to the Lord and releasing it to His hands. And how many times do we move without hesitation into something dangerous for us without looking once to see what God thinks about it?

We knew our precious little Sammy was in no danger from the storm, but he could never understand that. Some of us are like that too. How many of us take medicine to calm our fears when God wants us to trust Him to protect us? I am not saying that taking medicine is bad, or that people should never take medicine to calm their fears, or that people should immediately get off the medicine they are taking. I am saying that God wants to calm our fears, and we must trust Him enough to let Him do that—even if it begins one small step at a time.

The Bible says, "A thousand may fall at your side, and ten thousand at your right hand; but it shall not come near you...*Because you have made the LORD, who is my refuge, even the Most High, your dwelling place,* no evil shall befall you, nor shall any plague come near your dwelling" (Psalm 91:7,9-10).

The key to finding freedom from fear is making God your dwelling place.

If you make God the One in whom you put your total trust—and you take all your cares and needs to Him, walk closely with Him every day, and seek Him constantly—then He will give you a place of shelter in Him. The closer you draw to Him and His kingdom, the more you move into a place of safety from the storm under the umbrella of His protection.

Trust God to Hear and Answer Your Prayers

Every time you pray you demonstrate your love for God by declaring your humble dependence on Him.

Jesus said, "When you pray, go into your room, and when you have shut your door, *pray to your Father who is in the secret place;* and your Father who sees in secret will reward you openly" (Matthew 6:6).

As we *wait on God for His answer to our prayers,* He takes us out of our shaky situation and establishes us on a rock. He puts a song of praise in our heart, and when people see that, they are drawn to Him because of it. David said, "*I waited patiently for the LORD; and He inclined to me, and heard my cry. He also brought me up out of a horrible pit*, out of the miry clay, *and set my feet upon a rock*, and *established my steps*. He has put a new song in my mouth—praise to our God; many will see it and fear, and will trust in the LORD" (Psalm 40:1-3).

Waiting on the Lord after we have prayed is another way we show love for God.

In adoption some places take away the old birth certificate and give the orphan a new one with their new father's and mother's names on it. God does that for us too. When you are born again, your name is written in the book of life in heaven. God becomes your heavenly Father. You have a new life. A new identity. You are not the same old you. So don't keep thinking of yourself as having the same old identity.

When we don't understand that with God a process is going on as we pray, then we don't have patience to wait for the process. We jump to conclusions about whether God is answering our prayers or not. That shows a lack of trust in His ability to do a new thing in us.

I am not the same person who never got her prayers answered; I am a new creation in Christ. I'm not the same person who made stupid choices; I am a person who has the Spirit of wisdom in me. I am not the same person who had everything go wrong in her life; I am a new person who serves the God who makes all things right.

Trust God that He can change anything—including you.

Waiting on God means we are putting our total faith in Him. It means when we pray we are trusting that He hears us and will answer in His way and time. It means we are looking to Him and not losing heart. The Bible says, "I would have lost heart, unless I had believed that I would see the goodness of the LORD in the land of the living. *Wait on the LORD; be of good courage, and He shall strengthen your heart;* wait, I say, on the LORD!" (Psalm 27:13-14).

When you are tormented with doubt about whether God is who He says He is, or if He really cares about you, or will He really hear your prayers, or does He love you enough to rescue and protect you, it reveals a lack of trust in Him. But when you decide to trust Him at all times, He gives you strength in your heart and the ability to wait on Him in the process.

The Bible says that it is *because* you love God that He hears you when you pray. *"Because he has set his love upon Me, therefore I will deliver him;* I will set him on high, because he has known My name. *He shall call upon Me, and I will answer him; I will be with him in trouble; I will deliver him and honor him"* (Psalm 91:14-15).

God doesn't say we will never have problems. He says He will be with us to lift us up and protect us when we go through difficulties *because we love Him.*

You express your love for God when you trust Him in all things. Thinking you don't need Him except in an emergency or crisis does not please Him. You show love for God when you recognize your own weakness and dependence upon Him. It tells God that you don't want to even try to make it through a day without Him. Declaring your dependence upon God, and your love for Him, sets your priorities straight and makes them clear—not only to God, but also to you.

Loving and trusting God means not just praying when you are in a crisis, but as a way of life.

When something bad happens, deliberately tell yourself to put your hope in God to bring good out of it. Take your eyes off of your situation and look to Him. Don't give up hope, no matter what the outcome appears to be. Don't let the enemy's taunts cause you to doubt God's Word. Say, "Lord, I surrender my life to You today and everything in it—good or bad—knowing You will bring good out of each situation that is committed to You."

When we put our expectation in God knowing He is the *only one* we can always depend on, and when we completely trust in Him and wait on Him for help, we show our love for Him.

And in the process of expressing our love for God, we are transformed.

Prayer of *Love*

LORD, I put my trust in You. I quiet my soul and wait for You to be my defense, and I will not allow myself to be moved or shaken (Psalm 62:1-2). Reveal any place in my heart where I am afraid to do that fully. Help me to put You first in everything I do—day and night. I pray to You as David did, "Give heed to the voice of my cry, my King and my God, for to You I will pray. My voice You shall hear in the morning, O LORD; in the morning I will direct it to You, and I will look up" (Psalm 5:2-3). Thank You that You hear my prayers and will answer.

Help me to always look to You and not focus on my problems. Teach me to "pray without ceasing" (1 Thessalonians 5:17). My soul waits on You for answers to my prayers, because You are my help and shield (Psalm 33:20). I know that You will strengthen my heart when I put my hope in You (Psalm 31:24). I know there is peace to be found in any trial when I invite Your presence into it. Enable me to keep praying and seeking that peace in You until I have found it.

Lord, I thank You that Your thoughts toward me "are more than can be numbered" (Psalm 40:5). I am constantly grateful that You love me. "Show me Your ways, O LORD; teach me Your paths...on You I wait all the day" (Psalm 25:4-5). I lift my eyes to You for You are my help, and I know that You will not allow me to fall (Psalm 121:1,3). Enable me to put my complete trust in You at all times no matter what is happening.

In Jesus' name I pray.

Words of *Love*

You will keep him in perfect peace,
whose mind is stayed on You,
because he trusts in You.

Isaiah 26:3

Trust in the LORD with all your heart,
and lean not on your own understanding;
in all your ways acknowledge Him,
and He shall direct your paths.

Proverbs 3:5-6

Give ear, O LORD, to my prayer;
and attend to the voice of my supplications.
In the day of my trouble I will call upon You,
for You will answer me.

Psalm 86:6-7

My soul, wait silently for God alone,
for my expectation is from Him.
He only is my rock and my salvation;
He is my defense; I shall not be moved.

Psalm 62:5-6

Why are you cast down, O my soul?
And why are you disquieted within me?
Hope in God, for I shall yet praise Him
for the help of His countenance.

Psalm 42:5

12

Lean on
His Wisdom Enthusiastically

God is a good God who loves us. We must never allow the bad things that happen in life to cause us to doubt that and undermine our faith in Him and His infinite wisdom.

When we go through difficult times, if we stay humble before God and wait on Him to reveal His purpose and plan in our situation, it shows we are trusting in His goodness and relying on His infinite wisdom. But when we find ourselves in the middle of something serious in our life and don't lean on Him, too often that's because we don't comprehend how solid and reliable the wisdom of God is.

His wisdom is perfect and worthy of our full trust. That's because God's Spirit of wisdom is in us and is perfect and unfailing. We must learn to trust Him more than we do.

We must embrace God's wisdom and lean on it in every situation, no matter what is happening or how bad things get.

Trust God to Always Do the Right Thing

From the story of Job it's clear we cannot always understand what God allows or is doing in our life—at least not by our own human thinking. But He is sovereign, all-knowing, and all-powerful, so we can trust Him to do the right thing all the time.

Some people may see the book of Job as only about God's judgment, but it's about His mercy. God's mercy and love for Job is evident in His preservation and restoration of Job's life. You may think, as I have, *I would rather not go through what Job did and just forego the later blessings.* I wouldn't want to lose my children even if I were to have more later. But this story is not about whether we would be willing to have all our children killed and lose everything. It's about whether we would still trust in God and His infinite wisdom if our worst fears came upon us.

It has been my experience, and from my knowledge of God's Word, that we will have suffering in our lifetime, and it's far better to trust in the wisdom of God in these times than to blame Him for whatever we have to endure.

God's love can be found in our suffering as well as our blessings. "You have heard of *the perseverance of Job* and seen the end intended by the Lord—that *the Lord is very compassionate and merciful*" (James 5:11). God was not beating up on Job. His love for Job never wavered, just as His love for *us* never wavers. We must cling to this truth, especially when we are in the deepest pain of our life.

Job's friends—Eliphaz, Bildad, and Zophar—told Job he was suffering because he had sinned. They said people who sin are punished, so obviously Job was being punished. They thought a person's material blessings were evidence of God's favor and punishment was only in *this* life and not beyond their earthly lives. Job's response to his three friends was anger at them for accusing him instead of comforting him.

Job had not sinned. God said so.

God called Job "a blameless and upright man" (Job 1:8). This proves that we should all be careful about any rush to judgment over the reason for another believer's suffering.

Another person—Elihu—told Job that God was greater than man, and man did not have the right to question Him or require Him to explain His actions. He said that if we would be humble and listen, God would speak to us. He said Job needed to trust God in his suffering without requiring an explanation, and he needed to have a humble attitude toward God in the situation.

Job *did* have a humble attitude toward God. God said so.

The truth is, even good people are tested. We each have an *advocate* and an *adversary*.

Jesus is our *advocate*.

Satan is our *adversary*.

We battle our adversary by standing with our advocate in prayer. Job's suffering was Satan's idea. God allowed it (Job 2:3-6). Satan first destroyed Job's possessions and then killed his children, but *Job still worshipped God.* "Job arose, tore his robe, and shaved his head; and *he fell to the ground and worshiped.* And he said: 'Naked I came from my mother's womb, and naked shall I return there. The LORD gave, and the LORD has taken away; blessed be the name of the LORD'" (Job 1:20-21).

In all that happened Job did not sin. He never faulted God. *He worshipped Him!*

Then Satan attacked Job's body with painful boils. *But Job continued to worship God.* In the midst of his agony, Job did not blame God.

Job's wife advised, "Do you still hold fast to your integrity? Curse God and die!" (Job 2:9). But he said to her, "'You speak as one of the foolish women speaks. *Shall we indeed accept good from God, and shall we not accept adversity?*' In all this Job did not sin with his lips" (Job 2:10).

Job's wife lacked understanding or faith in God to bring restoration, so instead of comforting her husband she taunted and disrespected him. But Job did not curse God as Satan predicted he would. Instead, he cursed the day he was born and longed for death.

Job said, "Why is light given to him who is in misery, and life to the bitter of soul, who long for death, but it does not come?" (Job 3:20-21). He wondered why God didn't allow him to die as a way to end his agony.

Then Job said words we all pray we will never have cause to say. "My sighing comes before I eat, and my groanings pour out like water. *For the thing I greatly feared has come upon me, and what I dreaded has happened to me*" (Job 3:24-25).

The truth for us is that even if our own greatest fear comes upon us, and the very thing we dread happens, God will still make a way through it and bring restoration to us. The key is to trust and not blame God or become angry at Him. If we trust God in His wisdom to always do the right thing, we will be touched by His healing and restorative hand.

When God finally answered Job out of a whirlwind, He did not explain Job's suffering except to say that Job was not meant to know why. He was to understand that God cared about Job and his life, and that the suffering God allowed brought Job to the end of himself so he could find everything in the Lord.

God reprimanded Job's friends, saying they didn't speak the right thing to Job and they had to repent for that. He said to Eliphaz, "My wrath is aroused against you and your two friends, for you have not spoken of Me what is right, as My servant Job has" (Job 42:7). God accepted Job's faithfulness and instructed him to pray for Eliphaz, Bildad, and Zophar (Job 42:8).

It was when Job had *prayed for his faithless friends* that God restored all he had lost—sons and daughters, grandchildren, and possessions. "The LORD gave Job twice as much as he had before" (Job 42:10). Job had to pray for those who had given bad counsel and caused him more grief.

Job proved that he would not turn away from God in a time of adversity, as Satan said he would, but Job's suffering was directly from the devil. Before you start getting worried about the devil's power to destroy, remember that Jesus defeated Satan and all the powers of hell. At the mention of Jesus' name, and the knowledge that you are now in Christ, the enemy has to flee. The key is recognizing the enemy's attack and resisting his lies and temptations.

When the suffering was over, all of Job's brothers, sisters, and acquaintances came and ate with him in his house and comforted him. The Lord blessed the latter days of Job more than his beginning, and he had seven sons and three daughters, exactly what he had lost before (Job 42:10-13). Job lived 140 years and saw his children and grandchildren for four generations (42:16). God gave Job a wonderful and abundant life of total restoration.

The love of God is powerfully shown in Job's amazing story. Job thought his life was over and he looked forward to dying, but God had abundant life ahead for him. Job's love of God caused him to not turn away from God but toward Him, trusting in His wisdom.

Could you or I have trusted God after losing all of our children, all of our possessions, and our health? Yes, we could, but only if we had total love and trust for God's unfailing love, compassionate mercy, and infinite wisdom. If God in His wisdom, understanding, and knowledge founded the earth and the heavens, He can sustain us through anything if we continue to worship Him and not fault Him, love Him and not blame Him, and lean on His wisdom and not the wisdom of the world (Proverbs 3:19-20).

Reverence for God Is Where Our Wisdom Begins

There are two different kinds of wisdom. There is the *wisdom of the world* and the *wisdom of God*. We need to keep the distinction between the two perfectly clear in our mind at all times.

God's wisdom is the opposite of the world's. For example, the message of Jesus' suffering on the cross and His miraculous resurrection seems foolish to unbelievers, but to those of us who have been saved by what Jesus accomplished on the cross, we see it as the very power of God (1 Corinthians 1:18). God says that He "will destroy the wisdom of the wise" because the wisdom of this world does not know Him (1 Corinthians 1:19-21). Jesus is both the *power* of God *and* the *wisdom* of God, and that is why the world does not recognize Him. Earthly wisdom will come to nothing, but godly wisdom lasts forever.

We cannot depend on earthly wisdom. Paul said, "Your faith

should not be in the wisdom of men but in the power of God" (1 Corinthians 2:5).

When we depend on God's wisdom and not the world's, we cannot go wrong. Every time we seek God and ask His Spirit of wisdom to guide us, we are on solid ground. We can say, "I will bless the LORD who has given me counsel; my heart also instructs me in the night seasons. I have set the LORD always before me; because He is at my right hand I shall not be moved" (Psalm 16:7-8).

The Bible says, "*The fear of the Lord is the beginning of wisdom; a good understanding have all those who do His commandments*" (Psalm 111:10). Having reverence for God is the first step in receiving the wisdom of God, which is imparted to you by His indwelling Holy Spirit. That doesn't mean you know everything God knows. It means you will have godly wisdom you would not have without Him. It means you will have the wisdom to trust in God's infinite wisdom in your life.

True wisdom comes from God. The Bible says, "*Length of days is in her right hand, in her left hand riches and honor. Her ways are ways of pleasantness, and all her paths are peace. She is a tree of life* to those who take hold of her, and *happy are all who retain her*" (Proverbs 3:16-18). The wisdom God gives us brings long life, abundance, contentment, strength, peace, and happiness.

When we have godly wisdom, we walk safely, sleep soundly, and live unafraid. We have confidence knowing God will keep us from harm if we are wise enough to seek Him for everything, wise enough to hear His voice of wisdom speaking to our soul, wise enough to do the right thing. "Keep sound wisdom and discretion...*then you will walk safely in your way*, and *your foot will not stumble*. When you lie down, *you will not be afraid*; yes, you will lie down and *your sleep will be sweet*" (Proverbs 3:21,23-24).

That same chapter says that when we walk with wisdom, we don't have to "*be afraid of sudden terror*, nor of trouble from the wicked when it comes; *for the LORD will be your confidence, and will keep your foot from being caught*" (verses 25-26). How often have we seen disaster happen to people who did not seek wisdom from God before they made an important decision? That doesn't have to happen.

What a comfort that is—not having to be afraid of sudden terror or attacks of evil people—because God will protect us when we lean on His wisdom and we trust the Spirit of wisdom within us. When we live in the fear of the Lord, reverencing Him and fearing what life would be without Him, we dwell safely and securely without having to live in fear of evil (Proverbs 1:33).

God wants you to seek wisdom, understanding, and discernment just as you would search for a great treasure (Proverbs 2:1). He wants you to "*incline your ear to wisdom,* and apply your heart to understanding," for only "then will you understand the fear of the LORD, and find the knowledge of God" (Proverbs 2:2,5).

This means we need to be enthusiastically sold out to the Lord so that there is nothing in us not dedicated to and owned by Him. When we have so much love and reverence for God that we are hesitant to do anything that would cause Him any displeasure, then we are beginning to get it. We are beginning to understand what the fear of the Lord is all about. It's loving and reverencing Him and leaning on His unfailing wisdom—both *toward* us and *in* us.

When we choose to walk in humility before the Lord, the wisdom of God manifests itself in us.

Prayer of *Love*

LORD, I love that Your wisdom is eternal, true, and always perfect. Help me to seek out and depend on Your wisdom every day. Holy Spirit of wisdom, fill me afresh with Your wisdom so that I can always hear Your wise counsel spoken to my heart. I depend on Your counsel for all things. Teach me to value all my days on earth so that I may gain a heart of wisdom (Psalm 90:12).

I know that the counsel of nations comes to nothing, but You bless the nation who proclaims You are Lord and who seeks Your wisdom—the people You have chosen for Your own inheritance (Psalm 33:11-12). Thank You that Your counsel stands forever (Psalm 33:11). I am grieved at how my nation has rejected Your godly wisdom. Bring us back to You, I pray. Only in You can we ever find the wisdom to make right decisions. I know that man, in the arrogance of his own wisdom, comes to destruction, but trust that Your wisdom can enable us to survive.

I praise and worship You. And I thank You that reverencing You is where Your wisdom in me begins. Help me to always love and value You far above all else. I seek Your wisdom above earthly wisdom, for I know that those who do that are blessed. I don't want to be like those who "hated knowledge and did not choose the fear of the LORD" for they could not enjoy Your presence and did not get their prayers answered (Proverbs 1:28-29). As for me, I lean totally, enthusiastically, and unwaveringly on Your wisdom because I love and trust You.

In Jesus' name I pray.

Words of *Love*

The fear of the LORD is the beginning of knowledge,
but fools despise wisdom and instruction.

PROVERBS 1:7

When wisdom enters your heart,
and knowledge is pleasant to your soul,
discretion will preserve you; understanding will keep you,
to deliver you from the way of evil.

PROVERBS 2:10-12

The mouth of the righteous speaks wisdom,
and his tongue talks of justice.
The law of his God is in his heart;
none of his steps shall slide.

PSALM 37:30-31

The LORD gives wisdom; from His mouth
come knowledge and understanding;
He stores up sound wisdom for the upright;
He is a shield to those who walk uprightly.

PROVERBS 2:6-7

Wisdom is better than rubies, and all the things
one may desire cannot be compared with her.

PROVERBS 8:11

13

Leave the
World of His Enemy Entirely

G od's enemy is *our* enemy. And *our* enemy is *God's* enemy.
God delivers us from *our* enemy when we separate ourselves from *His.*

When we welcome evil into our lives in any way, we welcome the enemy of God, and we need the power, wisdom, guidance, and help of the Holy Spirit in order to separate ourselves completely from that realm. That doesn't mean we should isolate ourselves from everyone who doesn't believe the way *we* do. It means we don't give the enemy an opening into our mind and life in any way.

We're never allowed to have one foot in each kingdom.

Jesus said, "The ruler of this world is coming, and *he has nothing in Me*" (John 14:30). This means that because Jesus was sinless, Satan had no authority over Him. If we surrender nothing of our lives to the enemy and everything to Jesus, the enemy has no authority over *us* either.

God wants us to live in the world, but we are not to align our heart with the world's system. That's because it is opposed to God's kingdom and rule and all that God is and does. As much as it is up to us, we must choose to allow only godly and faith-filled people, who live in God's truth, to be the *influencers* in our lives.

David said, "*My eyes shall be on the faithful of the land, that they may dwell with me*" (Psalm 101:6). We, too, should not spend the majority of our time with those who might influence us to pick up any of the enemy's ways.

If we *align our heart with evil* in any way, it will come back upon us in some negative consequence. But if we express love for God by *resisting evil* in our lives, God will be our defender.

Ask God to Deliver You from Evil

Jesus taught us to pray, "*Deliver us from the evil one.*"

David prayed, "*Deliver me, O LORD, from evil men*; preserve me from violent men, who plan evil things in their hearts...who have purposed to make my steps stumble" (Psalm 140:1-2,4).

We, too, must often pray, "Deliver us from evil" and "protect us from evil men." That's because the *enemy* of *God* will attack each one of us. Jesus knew that, and it's why He taught us to pray the way He did. I always pray that my children will be delivered from evil as well because the enemy will try to entice them.

Too many people are in denial about whether we have a spiritual enemy who opposes us. And bad things happen in people's lives who are either ignorant of the enemy and his tactics, or they have chosen to be unaware of his existence. Whatever their belief about that, it's not working.

Jesus teaches us to pray that the plans of the enemy will not succeed in our life.

We show our love for God by *praying against evil*. David prayed, "*Still my prayer is against the deeds of the wicked*" (Psalm 141:5). We can pray *for* things and we can pray *against* things. Make it a habit to pray against the encroachment of evil into your life and the lives of your loved ones.

Jesus destroyed the power of evil by His death and resurrection. But evil is still here. The Bible assures us that evil will not triumph over us as long as we *resist it. We must take authority* over it in Jesus' name and *refuse to align* ourselves with it. God did *not* say, "Pretend the devil doesn't exist and he will flee." He said, "*Resist* the devil and he will flee from you" (James 4:7). Do I believe a demon is behind every bush? No, but I believe countless demons are in too many places and too many people.

The enemy is not everywhere, although some days it may seem as though that is true. That's what the enemy wants us to think. The truth is, only God is omnipresent. However, the enemy will be where he is invited to be. God will be where *He* is invited to be, as well, but in far greater power than the enemy. We must be careful who and what our thoughts, words, and actions invite into our life.

Because Jesus delivered us from evil and its power, that means evil has no power over us—if we choose not to buy into it. We see people in the news who sell their souls to the dark side and are rewarded with worldly enticements, but their eternal future will be with the dark side as well.

We are not allowed to forget that fact.

We must choose to turn away from even any *hint* of the dark side and live in the light with Jesus because our future depends on it.

Love God by Keeping Your Heart Separate from the World

We are all in a spiritual war between God and His enemy, and the sooner we recognize that, the sooner we can become the prayer warriors God wants us to be. In this spiritual war, prayer is the way we battle the enemy. But we must first clearly make the distinction as to what aligns us with the enemy and what does not. David said, "Their sorrows shall be multiplied who hasten after another god" (Psalm 16:4). *Those who follow after the enemy will not have peace.*

We show love for God by separating ourselves from anything that separates us from Him. When we do that, God delivers us out of the grasp of the enemy's hands. "*You who love the LORD, hate evil! He preserves the souls of His saints; He delivers them out of the hand of the wicked*" (Psalm 97:10).

Evil constantly plots against us, and we must remember at all times to turn to God for help to win the battles we are in with the enemy. God *prepares* us for battle. He *teaches us how* to do battle against the enemy. He *delivers us* from our enemy. And He *gives us victory.*

God doesn't want us to only resist the enemy, to only try to defend ourselves against the plans of evil. He wants us to go on the *offensive* and pray for the destruction of the enemy's plans before he even attempts to execute them.

David said, *"It is God who arms me with strength, and makes my way perfect...*I have pursued my enemies and overtaken them; neither did I turn back again till they were destroyed" (Psalm 18:32,37). *God arms us and helps us in battle by enabling us to do what we cannot do without Him.*

God protects us from our enemy, and He *teaches us* to pray through the attacks against us and to not give up until our enemy is defeated. Even when our enemy surrounds us, we can call upon the Lord and His name alone will deliver us.

We must separate ourselves from those who reject God and His ways. The psalmist said, "My soul has dwelt too long with one who hates peace" (Psalm 120:6).

The enemy often disguises himself, even as a type of quasi-believer. That is how cults are formed. Their beliefs seem *kind of right*, or *mostly right*, or *could be right*. And they appeal to those who want to be the *most right* of anyone. Be suspicious of any group promising they alone have special revelation from God that no one else has, or that only they have true revelation from God. Cults are built and established on these kinds of claims, and the people in them become blinded to the truth.

We can all be enticed into the world of the enemy that way if we are not diligent to keep our heart clean before the Lord. Remember, *"The heart is deceitful above all things"* (Jeremiah 17:9). God said He searches our heart and tests our mind and rewards us according to what He finds (Jeremiah 17:10). There are those who *pretend* to be good, or *think* they are good but who are *not*, and God knows the truth about that.

Sometimes we are tested by God to see if we will join the wicked when they seem to be winning. For example, when the people around us serving evil are the popular ones, will we forsake God and align ourselves with them? We must never be weak in resisting evil. Every time we are faced with a choice, we must make the right one. And each day our choices must be clear. "The LORD tests the righteous, but the wicked and the one who loves violence His soul hates" (Psalm 11:5).

God tests those He loves. We show love for God by passing each test.

When we do as the Bible says and love the Lord with all of our heart, soul, and strength, then we won't fall for the lure of the enemy and will pass the test of whether we will resist him or not (Deuteronomy 6:5).

We have a choice every day as to what or who we lift up our souls to. Will it be an idol or will it be the Lord? David said, "To You, O LORD, I lift up my soul. O my God, I trust in You; *let me not be ashamed; let not my enemies triumph over me*" (Psalm 25:1-2). When we lift our soul to any form of idol, our enemy always triumphs.

Loving God means separating ourselves from the world's value system and instead valuing the things of God above all else. It means listening for the voice of God over all other voices—including the voice of our own self-interest.

Ask God frequently to show you if there is any idol in your life to which you have lifted up your soul. You may be surprised at what He shows you. Even judging ourselves by the world's image of how we should look or act can become an idol to us.

The Bible says we are not to "give place to the devil" (Ephesians 4:27). For example, if we truly love God, we will not look at things that are ungodly and opposed to His ways. When we do, it wounds *our spirit* and grieves *His*. If we fill our thoughts with the things of God, we will keep ourselves from allowing evil in. David said, "*I will set nothing wicked before my eyes*; I hate the work of those who fall away; it shall not cling to me. *A perverse heart shall depart from me*; I will not know wickedness" (Psalm 101:3-4). We must learn to say the same thing.

Even though David did at one point allow himself to think and view what was evil, it grieved him so painfully that he repented before God and paid an enormous price for his lack of judgment.

We have to make a conscious and ongoing effort to depart from all evil and do the right thing. Ask God to show you if there is anything in your life with which you have aligned your heart and from which you need to separate yourself. There is great freedom and relief when you do.

God never takes away our right to make bad choices. We have to choose to turn from living life on our own terms to living life on *His*.

Don't Be Overwhelmed When Evil Prospers

We all see evil proliferating in the world every day. And just when we think we've seen it all, something even more unimaginably horrific happens. We observe ruthless people benefiting from bad deeds and we wonder, *How long will evil reign and profit?*

David saw the same thing happening in his time and said, "*Do not fret because of evildoers, nor be envious of the workers of iniquity. For they shall soon be cut down like the grass, and wither as the green herb*" (Psalm 37:1-2). Isn't it comforting to know there will be an end to the evil we see? That's why we must never covet their profits.

We wonder why the wicked flourish, but the Bible says it is so they will be destroyed forever (Psalm 92:7). God gives them a chance to turn back to Him, but when they refuse it is clear where they stand. God's enemies *will* be destroyed because He is all-powerful, He will not be mocked, and He always has the last word (Psalm 92:8-9).

Instead of fretting over the evil, here are some things we can do in the meantime until the workers of evil are destroyed:

- ✧ *"Trust in the LORD, and do good;* dwell in the land, and feed on His faithfulness" (Psalm 37:3).

- ✧ *"Delight yourself also in the LORD,* and He shall give you the desires of your heart" (Psalm 37:4).

- ✧ *"Commit your way to the LORD,* trust also in Him, and He shall bring it to pass. He shall bring forth your righteousness as the light, and your justice as the noonday" (Psalm 37:5-6).

- ✧ *"Rest in the LORD, and wait patiently for Him;* do not fret because of him who prospers in his way, because of the man who brings wicked schemes to pass" (Psalm 37:7).

- ✧ *"Cease from anger,* and forsake wrath; do not fret—it only causes harm" (Psalm 37:8).

It's easy to let ourselves be overwhelmed by how evil is prospering today, but if we choose instead to trust in the Lord, do good and delight ourselves in Him, commit our lives to Him, rest and wait patiently for Him, and not let ourselves be consumed with anger, we will live with our mind, emotions, deepest thoughts, and spiritual self focused entirely on Him and loving Him with all our heart.

Our anger does not produce God's righteousness; only our love does.

In these days that are becoming more and more evil, draw even closer to God. Proclaim Him as your Lord and Master. Recognize all the good in your life and your world that would not exist without Him. Say, "You are my Lord, my goodness is nothing apart from You" (Psalm 16:2). Enjoy God's people. "As for the saints who are on the earth, they are the excellent ones, in whom is all my delight" (Psalm 16:3).

Don't covet what evil people acquire. "A little that a righteous man has is better than the riches of many wicked" (Psalm 37:16).

You have more important things to do.

God Has Delivered You from Fear of the Enemy

One of the reasons we have an enemy is *because* we are the Lord's. That's why we can not only ask God to deliver us from the enemy's evil plans, but also to keep us from even the *fear* of the enemy. David prayed, *"Preserve my life from fear of the enemy. Hide me from the secret plots of the wicked"* (Psalm 64:1-2).

David knew who was on his side. He said, "If it had not been the LORD who was on our side, when men rose up against us, then they would have swallowed us alive, when their wrath was kindled against us; then the waters would have overwhelmed us, *the stream would have gone over our soul"* (Psalm 124:2-4).

You need to know who is on your side too. It should never be that the fear of the enemy overwhelms your soul.

Remember this: God is all-powerful. He cannot create anything that is more powerful than He is. It's impossible. Don't be tricked by dumb questions about such things asked by people who want to make Christians look stupid. The enemy is nowhere near as powerful as God and never will be. The enemy's power comes only by people believing his lies instead of *God's truth.*

Because we love God, we choose to serve *Him* and not the enemy. David said, "The LORD is my light and my salvation; whom shall I fear? *The LORD is the strength of my life; of whom shall I be afraid?...* *Though an army may encamp against me, my heart shall not fear*; though war may rise against me, in this I will be confident" (Psalm 27:1,3).

David knew God would hide and protect him.

The enemy will always try to stop everything the Lord wants to do in you and in your life. Don't be afraid. Hide yourself in the Lord in prayer, worship, and in His Word. If the attack on you is big, your blessing on the other side of it will surely be big as well. The challenges you face moving into the promised land of where God is leading you will work in you the faith and strength to thrive in it. Our weakest moments can precede God's greatest work in our lives.

These times of enemy attack will only increase your trust in the Lord and the peace He gives you.

God Will Protect You from the Purveyors of Evil

Jesus triumphed over the enemy. Now the power in you is greater than the power of evil.

Yes, there have been evil things done by people who called themselves Christians—such as in the Holocaust and slavery—but those were not Christians. They were not people who received Jesus and all that He did on the cross, and were filled with the Spirit of wisdom, comfort, and love that Jesus gives those who love Him. They did not love God above all else and seek to be led by Him every day.

Not even close!

The people who did those things were not empowered and moved by the love of God. The fragrance and beauty of the Lord was not in them. They were lovers of themselves and purveyors of evil. They sold their hearts to the enemy of God and His ways and served the enemy and themselves entirely. There is no excuse or justification for it that even remotely aligns itself with God in any way. It is in stark and brutal opposition to all that God is. What they did is ugly and has the stench of evil.

Godly people are motivated by God's love in what they do. Evil people reveal themselves by their lack of love.

You can always tell the people who are standing on a foundation of straw in their beliefs—who have left God out of their "religions" by the way they attack God, Jesus, and the Holy Spirit. They vilify believers, they mock God, and they turn all their efforts toward destroying God's name and His people. Not all religions are the same. You can't lump them all together and say they are all bad or all good. That reveals the immense ignorance of those who do that. But you can look around you, and if you see that a person, or a group of people, is trying to destroy those who don't believe the way they do, then you will understand that they are on shaky ground in their belief system. They know it, and that's why they have to destroy those who are not with them. You see that cruelty in dictators and leaders of false religions.

Check out those who try to destroy all knowledge of God. When you identify such people who do that, they are always godless. They are serving the evil and dark realm.

People who serve the dark side have to eliminate those who serve in the light. When you see people trying to eliminate anyone who disagrees or opposes them, that is a sign they are serving the dark and evil side and serving up a lie for their own benefit. They believe that in order for them to rule and prevail, they must eliminate the truth.

Just as the law of gravity is true everywhere, so are God's laws. Natural laws are set up by God, and His laws are true in every country and town. It is always wrong to violate any of His laws and commands because consequences are built into them. If you see a people rejecting God's laws as stated in the Bible, they are not of God.

God created you with a will, and you must make choices as to who you will and will not serve. Whether you think so or not, you will serve the dark forces of evil if you are not deliberately and actively serving the Lord. Not believing in the Lord puts you in an unbelieving fog. You don't see anything straight. You are influenced most by the loudest voice defying God.

But if you love and serve God, and express your love for Him by separating yourself from all evil and resisting the advance of evil in prayer and action, you are protected. You do not need to fear being bought off by the enemy in any way when you are already sold out to God.

Prayer of *Love*

LORD, help me to express my love for You by separating myself completely from anything that is not pleasant in Your sight. If the enemy of my soul has anything in me, reveal it to me now so I can be free of any influence he may have. If I have in any way attached my heart or thoughts to his ways—or have been drawn away from Your kingdom—show me so I can repent of it and come back to You and under Your protective covering.

Enable me to stand strong in resisting the enemy so he will flee from me. I will not look to any person to be my savior "for the help of man is useless" if not led by You (Psalm 108:12). Against the enemy, no one can do what You do. That's why my eyes are always on You (Psalm 25:15). Thank You, Jesus, that You have defeated the enemy and put him under Your feet. Help me to take up the shield of faith in You that protects me from enemy attack (Ephesians 6:16). "For Your righteousness' sake bring my soul out of trouble. In Your mercy cut off my enemies, and destroy all those who afflict my soul; for I am Your servant" (Psalm 143:11-12).

Help me to resist all temptation to live as those who serve the enemy. When tempted, I will worship You because praise invites Your presence in a powerful way and the enemy hates it. Thank You that You are on my side and I need not fear what man can do to me (Psalm 118:6). Thank You that Your commandments "make me wiser than my enemies" (Psalm 119:98). Thank You that no weapon of the enemy formed against me will prosper (Isaiah 54:17).

In Jesus' name I pray.

Words of *Love*

When the enemy comes in like a flood,
the Spirit of the LORD will lift up a standard against him.

ISAIAH 59:19

By this I know that You are well pleased with me,
because my enemy does not triumph over me.
As for me, You uphold me in my integrity, and set me
before Your face forever.

PSALM 41:11-12

Whatever is born of God overcomes the world.
And this is the victory that has overcome the world—
our faith. Who is he who overcomes the world, but he
who believes that Jesus is the Son of God?

1 JOHN 5:4-5

For yet a little while and the wicked shall be no more…
But the meek shall inherit the earth, and shall delight
themselves in the abundance of peace.

PSALM 37:10-11

When I cry out to You, then my enemies will turn back;
this I know, because God is for me.

PSALM 56:9

14

Long for His Will and His Presence Continuously

~~~~~~

Something happens to our mind, soul, and spirit when we come to the point where we not only long for a deeper level of relationship with God but know we can't live without it. We finally realize that only He can fill the empty space in us and don't want to waste any more of our time looking in other places. We come to the end of ourselves and don't want to live one moment outside of His will. We've already tried that and proven it doesn't work.

Once we've made that major decision to go deeper with the Lord and there is no turning back, our lives will never be the same. We know too much to question His absolute importance in our life.

At this point there are two things you must have:

1. The knowledge that you are living in the center of God's will.
2. The sense that you are in His presence.

Having this knowledge and sense every day is like food for your soul. It feeds you with a fullness only He can give you. When we love God enough to want His presence and perfect will in our lives at all times, it's because we understand that if we don't have that, then we are not as close to Him as we can be.

We Show Love for God by Longing to Be in His Perfect Will

Life is short. Forever is a long time. That's why we must desire nothing beyond God's will for us. And we should settle for nothing less either.

God is a God who can be known.

That means His *will* can be known as well.

Jesus said, "My food is to do the will of Him who sent Me" (John 4:34). Like Jesus, we must long for God's will to be done in our lives just as we long for food. Our love for God is shown by our *desire* to live in His will, and knowing that doing His will is more satisfying than anything else.

We show love for God by looking to Him for direction and not presuming we know what His will is concerning the certain specifics of our lives. We all know from His Word that He doesn't want us to lie, steal, or commit murder. This is true for everyone. But does He want us to quit our job and move to Tennessee? He might want *you* to do that, but that may not be God's will for everyone else. You must know His will about that for you.

When you need to know the will of God about your life specifically, the only way to understand it is to pray, pray, pray. And then pray with other people whose walk with God is deep and true, who love God more than all else.

When we do not live in God's will, or we have stepped outside of it, it's not so much that God slaps us down as punishment but that we have forfeited the blessings that were ours if we were *in* God's will. Living outside the boundaries of God's will by not living in a way that pleases Him exposes us to the very consequences we want to avoid.

That's why we must draw near to God and seek to know His will every day. We must search His Word for it and we must pray for it.

Too often people wait to seek God's will until something terrible happens—such as a tragedy or calamity. Or it may take a severe difficulty to wake us up to the fact that we have slidden away from God's perfect will, where we once were. We have let our heart toward God become weak, insipid, timid, toxic, variable, or indifferent. But because He is merciful and loves us, the moment we turn back from our wayward slipping away and seek Him with a truly repentant and humble heart, He forgives us and receives us back under the protective umbrella of His perfect will.

We can't presume to know God's will in all things without asking Him.

Presumption is having an attitude toward something that is not accurate. It is failing to listen for a word from God because you think you already know what His direction will be, but it's not correct. Presumption leads us to have false confidence because we believe something to be true that doesn't really exist. We have confidence that a certain thing is God's will when it really isn't.

When Jerusalem fell to its enemy, many of the Israelites were carried away captive. Those who were left asked Jeremiah to pray that they would have clear direction as to whether they should go to Egypt or stay where they were.

Jeremiah said, "I will pray to the LORD your God according to your words, and it shall be, that whatever the LORD answers you, I will declare it to you. I will keep nothing back from you" (Jeremiah 42:4).

But even though Jeremiah had favor with God, it still took ten days to receive the answer from Him, which was that they were to stay in Jerusalem.

However, the Israelites had already made up their minds that they were going to Egypt no matter what. They either presumed to know God's will or they didn't care what His will was for them. Either way, it was a horrible choice.

Because they did not wait on God for *His* direction, the people were destroyed. It is said of Jerusalem that "*she did not consider her destiny*; therefore her collapse was awesome; she had no comforter" (Lamentations 1:9).

These people didn't consider their destiny because they didn't care about what God wanted. They wanted what *they* wanted instead. And they wanted it right then. Waiting on God for the answer was not in their mind at that point.

Far too many of us have done things of which it can be said that we did not consider our destiny when we did them. How many times in your life have you done something without truly thinking through the consequences? Not many if you relied on God's wisdom and leading, and you sought the knowledge of His perfect will. But I'm talking about *before* that. Before you knew to value God's Word and His wisdom and His will. How many do-overs would you like to have if you had a time machine? I can think of so many things in my life that it's scary. Thank God for His mercy that causes us to rise above our mistakes and lack of judgment. Thank God that He can make things right, healed, or restored. Where would we be without His redemption and restoration?

The way to have a life without those kinds of regrets is to live in His will and refuse to live any other way. When you've had a big gulp of what it's like to *not* be in God's will, and the taste is so bitter that you want to do anything to avoid having to drink from that cup ever again, then you will do whatever it takes to never be outside God's will—even for a moment.

We Show Love for God by Making the Right Choices

While it's true you can read God's Word to find out what His will is concerning most of your life, there are choices you must make, and you need to hear from God specifically regarding them. We cannot assume we know His will without hearing from Him and getting His peace about it. We can't assume God will do things a certain way because that's what He did in the past. We can't try to force God into a box of our design. We cannot presume to know what He is saying without asking Him what His will is in that particular situation.

God wants us to walk with Him, keep our eyes on Him, listen for His voice leading us, and seek to know His will every moment. He doesn't want us running off on our own, thinking we have Him all figured out and we know as much as He does, so we don't need to check with Him anymore. And He definitely doesn't want us doing what the Israelites did—deciding to do what *we* want to do regardless of what *God* wants.

Not considering our destiny has disastrous consequences.

We must have a heart that truly listens for God to speak His will to us. And we cannot have selective hearing—only hearing as much as we want to hear and when we are ready to hear it.

Not listening to God will always cost us, and the price will always be too high.

Jesus said, "I have come down from heaven, *not to do My own will, but the will of Him who sent Me*" (John 6:38). Even Jesus sought God in order to do His heavenly Father's will.

We show love for God by longing for His will. But that means being completely honest with Him. If we come to Him with less than perfect motives, we will wonder why He doesn't answer our prayers.

Some people believe if you say anything negative about yourself it is a sign of unbelief. Therefore you cannot say "I'm sick," or "I'm afraid," or "I'm sad." To do so would be giving in to it—even to speak of it in prayer. But I say if you don't speak the truth in prayer, you don't really give God a chance to answer. Then it is *you* doing it. The psalmist said, "I believed, therefore I spoke, 'I am greatly afflicted'" (Psalm 116:10). Because he believed in God, he spoke the truth about himself and his affliction.

It's best to pray, "Lord, this is what is happening to me, and this is what I want to see happen in this situation, but more than that, I want what *You* want."

I have known friends who died from their ailments who would not even ask people to pray for them because they would have to confess they were sick. God's healing is an act of His mercy upon us. It's not something we *make happen* because of our great faith. *God* decides whom He heals and when it's our time to die. We have to let God be God and not try to make things happen without His power.

God's will is not all about us. He has things He wants to do in this world, and He wants to use each of us as His instruments to do them. He doesn't need us. He can do what He does by Himself, but He chooses to *partner with us* to do His will on earth. We cannot fulfill our calling if we are not first of all seeking His will for our life.

You have to be honest when you seek to know God's will about a specific thing that's personal to you. Tell Him how you feel about it, but let Him know you want what *He* wants more than anything else. When you seek His will for every part of your life, you will be amazed at what doors open up for you to do His will for others.

We Show Love for God by Longing for His Presence

We must develop a passion for the presence of God. We do that by growing into a passion for Jesus, a passion for His Spirit in us, a passion to serve and please Him, and a passion for the Word of God.

Once you sense God's presence in your life, you will long for it every day. You will always desire to live in that peaceful place. When you long for His presence more than anything else, you won't want to go back to living any other way. Anything less is no longer acceptable. You will be hopelessly addicted to His presence, and hopefully you will never recover from it.

Moses warned the Israelites not to go into the Promised Land, which the Lord had promised to them, because it was too late. They had already failed to trust God when He asked them to go in earlier. They had their chance and they totally blew it. But now they were *presuming* this was what God still wanted them to do without checking with Him first.

Moses said, "Why do you transgress the command of the LORD? For this will not succeed" (Numbers 14:41). He warned them that they would be defeated by their enemies *because the Lord was no longer with them* (Numbers 14:42).

The Israelites had lost God's presence with them because of their lack of faith and their disobedience. Can there be anything sadder in our lives than to lose the presence of God once we have it?

Moses said, "You shall fall by the sword; because you have turned away from the LORD, *the Lord will not be with you*" (Numbers 14:43). But they ignored what Moses said and did what they wanted to do. As a result, their enemies attacked them and drove them away.

We lose the closeness of God's presence when we don't seek Him above all else, and we violate His ways by living outside of His will. But when we submit our spirit to Him and welcome a fresh sense of His Spirit in us every day, and seek His guidance in all things, *He empowers us to do the right thing.*

God does not promise us a continual rose garden, nor does He say our lives will always be a living hell. He says we will have trials, but we can find joy and peace in the midst of them as we seek His presence in the situation we are in.

There is a movement out in Christendom among reactionaries to the prosperity gospel. The supporters of the prosperity gospel believe a person can claim anything they want and God will give it to them. The reactionaries to that belief system have gone to the other extreme and claim there is a misery and suffering gospel, as if that is all we can ever hope for on earth. It has become heresy to them that anyone could ever find happiness or joy this side of heaven. I don't believe in either of these extremes, and neither should you. I don't see the case for either side in the Bible. God gives happiness *and* also allows suffering for His purposes. And to claim we will never experience one or the other is wrong. It's like putting God in a box and dictating to Him what He can or cannot do.

God is not like a genie who, when you snap your spiritual fingers in prayer, will appear and make everything right. He is not Santa Claus, nor is He a dictator. He is the God of love, peace, and joy who wants us to put our trust in Him. God wants us to seek Him intensely, long for Him deeply, pour out our love for Him in praise and worship lavishly, devour His Word like food for our soul, and stop trying to control what He does in our lives. It's the least we can do considering all He has done for us.

Living in God's Presence Brings You into Your Destiny

Jesus instructed us to first seek God's kingdom, and then we will have everything we need (Matthew 6:33). In other words, seek God in prayer and in His Word and refuse to worry about the future. That doesn't mean don't think about *planning* for the future, or *working* for the future; it means we do what God asks and *trust Him* for the future.

Seeking God first will always put us in the correct position and aim us in the right direction to move into the future God has for us.

God says the future He has for us is good.

Making God a priority by letting Him know every day how much you need Him, and that you are keeping your eyes on Him, and you are walking with Him through every step of your life will keep you on the path that leads to the future He has for you.

You must decide to trust Him and "be anxious for nothing, but *in everything by prayer and supplication, with thanksgiving,* let your requests be made known to God" (Philippians 4:6). The promise here is that when you release the situation you are concerned about into God's hands in prayer, then *"the peace of God, which surpasses all understanding,* will guard your hearts and minds through Christ Jesus" (Philippians 4:7). What a wonderful promise to us. We get peace in exchange for praying and trusting God.

He will show us the right way to go, but we have to be looking to Him to see what that is. God says, "I will instruct you and teach you in the way you should go; *I will guide you with My eye*" (Psalm 32:8).

When our son was a child, he had to be clearly disciplined in order for him to do the right thing. With our daughter, all my husband or I had to do was give her a look of disapproval and that took care of the matter. That's because she was looking to see what our reaction was. Our son was not even thinking about looking to see that. He was busy doing what seemed like a good idea at the time. He had to be taught to look to us for guidance.

We, too, must be looking to God for His approval of what we do. That means having a sensitive heart toward Him and frequently turning to Him to see if what we are doing pleases Him. We don't want to be like a wild horse that cannot be tamed without a bit and bridle. We want to be sensitive to the Lord. We will save ourselves a lot of grief if we do that because mercy surrounds those of us who trust in God, and we are guaranteed to have joy (Psalm 32:9-11).

That's good enough reason for me. What about you?

Prayer of *Love*

LORD, I long to do Your will at all times. Doing Your will is food for my mind, soul, and spirit that gives me strength and peace. I don't ever want to be outside of Your perfect will for my life, so help me to always look to You for guidance and counsel. Lord Jesus, I know You did not seek Your own will on earth, but the will of Your Father who sent You (John 5:30). Enable me to fully submit my will to our heavenly Father as well. Lord, I pray You will always fill me with the knowledge of Your perfect will (Colossians 1:9).

You are life to me, and I cannot live without sensing Your presence in my life. "I spread out my hands to You; my soul longs for You like a thirsty land" (Psalm 143:6). I know that "the upright shall dwell in Your presence" (Psalm 140:13). Help me to do the right thing so that I don't lose that sense of Your presence. I am grateful You never leave or forsake me because Your Spirit dwells within me, but I don't want to do anything to grieve Your Spirit in me or to lose my sense of closeness to You.

Lord, I know there is a connection between living in Your perfect will and sensing Your presence in my life. I know You are everywhere, but the closeness of Your presence is only felt by those who draw close to You and seek to do Your will. Enable me to never sacrifice the closeness of Your presence because of wanting things my way instead of Yours. I submit my life to You.

In Jesus' name I pray.

Words of *Love*

The world is passing away, and the lust of it;
but he who does the will of God abides forever.

1 JOHN 2:17

Do not be unwise, but understand
what the will of the Lord is.

EPHESIANS 5:17

Do not be conformed to this world,
but be transformed by the renewing of your mind,
that you may prove what is that good and acceptable
and perfect will of God.

ROMANS 12:2

Not everyone who says to Me, "Lord, Lord,"
shall enter the kingdom of heaven,
but he who does the will of My Father in heaven.

MATTHEW 7:21

As the deer pants for the water brooks,
so pants my soul for You, O God.
My soul thirsts for God, for the living God.

PSALM 42:1-2

Third Choice

Choose to Love Others

in a Way That
Pleases God

15

Is Consistently Loving Others Really Possible?

No one could love you more or better than God does. You can't resist His unconditional, unfailing love for long once you fully understand it. Born out of that understanding, a deep and abiding love for *Him* develops within you. And the way you express your love for God affects who you become. It's in the very process of showing your love for God that He pours His love into you.

Once you sense your own love for God in response to His love for you, you want to show it to Him in every way possible. One of the most important ways to express your love for God is to love others. And this is the third choice we need to must make. In fact, loving God is not complete without it. Choosing to love others fulfills our calling and purpose and clarifies the reason we are here. The Bible says, "*If God so loved us, we also ought to love one another*" (1 John 4:11).

Though you may think I'm assuming you don't know how to love others on your own, that's not true. I know you're able to do that, just as I knew I was. But we all tend to place limits on ourselves in that regard and draw up boundaries in our life that are not established by God. Once He gave me that profound revelation while reading the love chapter in the Bible (1 Corinthians 13), I realized I didn't know how to love others with a depth and consistency that fully pleases Him. That's the way He loves *us*.

I could love my children, of course. Who doesn't? But I could withhold love from people who hurt me. And I could love from afar those who violated my trust. That's because I was trying to love them without God's help. In fact, it's impossible to love others the way God wants us to without His *enablement*.

It's with the love God pours into us that we can love others.

Without the Holy Spirit guiding us every day, we can still act in a loveless manner toward even those we love. But with *God's love in us, it's possible to love even our loved ones better.*

Every situation we encounter requires a choice on our part as to whether we sow love into it. And we can only make the right choice by the Spirit's leading in response to our prayers. If we are willing to look to Him, God will help us show love in each situation and with each person.

The truth is, God wants us to spend enough time with Him so that we develop His heart of love for others. He invites us to come to Him every day to receive a fresh, new flow of His Spirit of love in us. Because God *is* love—and His Spirit of love is *in* us—we are able to love in a way that pleases Him.

Our love for others is the most important sign that we know God and have been spiritually born into His kingdom.

Love is one of the fruit of the Spirit. "The fruit of the Spirit is love, joy, peace, longsuffering, kindness, goodness, faithfulness, gentleness, self-control" (Galatians 5:22-23). Each one of these manifesting through us is a sign that we have the Holy Spirit in us.

No one has actually seen God, but when we show love for others, they see His heart. That's the way I first saw God's love—through the love of believing friends and their pastor. "No one has seen God at any time. *If we love one another, God abides in us, and His love has been perfected in us*" (1 John 4:12). I came to the Lord because I sensed love I had never seen before. But that was only the beginning.

God reveals Himself to others through the love He pours *in* and *through* us to them. People may come to the Lord because of the love we extend to them.

During Jesus' time on earth, people were attracted to His love. They loved His miracles, of course, but it was more than that. Jesus showed love to all who had a heart for Him and His heavenly Father. He may have seemed harsh with those whose heart was hard against God, but He was revealing who and what they were and the idols and false gods they served.

Paul told us to *"walk in love, as Christ also has loved us and given Himself for us"* (Ephesians 5:2). The apostle John said, *"Let us love one another, for love is of God; and everyone who loves is born of God and knows God"* (1 John 4:7).

Those who don't respond to love are usually afraid to trust it because they have been burned by what they thought was love in the past. But that was inconsistent, shallow, or fake love. It wasn't true love. It was halfhearted attempts at human love at its worst. Or it was no love at all. True love originates from God and manifests itself in those who know Him.

Without Love as Our Motivation, We Accomplish Nothing

No matter how eloquently we speak, if we don't have love in our heart, our words mean nothing (1 Corinthians 13:1). When interacting with people, the words we say will not accomplish anything if not spoken in love. If we could speak every language on earth but don't have a love language to accompany our words, they will just be noise (1 Corinthians 13:1). We can say the kindest words to someone, but if we don't have love in our heart, they fall lifeless to the ground.

We can manifest great spiritual gifts, have superior knowledge, and display faith strong enough to move mountains, but all of that will accomplish nothing if we do it without love (1 Corinthians 13:2).

The basis of all spiritual gifts is love. If someone claims to have— or appears to have—spiritual gifts of any kind but doesn't exhibit the love of God, those gifts are meaningless. We can evaluate the motivating spirit of anyone on the basis of whether they reveal the love of God working in and through them. Any manifestation of spiritual gifts that doesn't also manifest the love of God is suspect.

Only what we do out of pure love lasts forever. All else is temporary.

We could go to the extreme of giving away everything we have to feed, clothe, and house the poor, or we could sacrifice ourselves in the most heroic of ways, even our body or our life, but if we don't do those things out of a heart of pure love, they won't profit us in any way (1 Corinthians 13:3).

Love is what gives meaning to all that we do.

Everyone needs to know God still loves them. They don't want to be constantly reminded of all they do wrong. We believers have the key to life in that we can communicate the love of God to them, but too often what is actually communicated by some is judgment, and it becomes a weapon against others. They think they can get people to change by shaming them and using their failures as evidence against them. This tactic is way wrong and *does not work*.

I didn't come to the Lord because a Christian told me what a miserable failure I was. I received the Lord because they told me God loves me. And they extended His love toward me in a way I clearly felt and trusted. I knew this love I sensed was far greater than any human love.

If we really love people we will tell them God loves them. We will explain how He has made a way for them to stay out of hell. We will explain to them how to have eternal life with the Lord and a better life here and now.

People want to know that *you* love them too. And one of the best ways to show your love to others is to share how much God loves them. Even if you don't feel like sharing that at the moment, remember that it's not about you anyway. Well, not entirely. It's about *God filling you with His love* and leading you to *touch other people* with it in a life-changing way. And in the process of sharing the love of God with others, He changes *you.*

The more you show love to others with the love God has given you, the more you will be changed into the likeness of God.

We Must Respond to Jesus' Great Commandment

Jesus told us we are to live in His love by keeping His commandments, and when we do that we will find joy (John 15:9-11). Our greatest priority in loving Him is to obey His commandment to *"love one another"* as He loves us (John 15:12). Jesus proved His love for us by suffering unbearable torture and an agonizing death and taking the consequences of our collective sins on Himself. Could you or I make such a sacrifice? Is God requiring that from us? No. That's because He already did it. It's done. He accomplished it.

We don't have to do what Jesus did, but He *is* asking us to lay down our lives for Him by loving others. And we are far from effective in doing that without the enablement of His Holy Spirit. He, after all, is the one who pours God's love into us when we open our hearts up to Him. But we should always be led by Him in the ways we show His love—now our love also—to others.

We Show Love for Others When We Pray for Them

The first and best way to show love for others is by praying for them. Prayer is one of our greatest gifts of love to people, and most of us don't give it often enough. We can be stingy in that way. It is a gift we *always* have with us, and while it has great value, it costs us only a small amount of time.

The truth is, we grow to love those for whom we wholeheartedly pray.

Amazing things happen when we pray for others, and it not only happens for them but for *us* as well. Every time we pray for someone, God gives us His heart of love for that person. That's because we are spending time with the God of love, and there is a remarkable transference of love between His heart and ours.

The closer you walk with God and the more time you spend with Him, the sooner your heart aligns with His until His heart of love becomes yours as well.

God wants us to love people enough to tell them about Him, but we must pray first for an open heart in that person. Or that we know the appropriate time. We can't wait for what seems like the *perfect* time because that may never come. And what seems like an imperfect time to us may be the perfect time in God's eyes. That's why we have to ask Him to lead us to who needs to be touched by His love. Rushing in to speak to someone without prayer can do more damage than good.

Love Our Enemies Too? You've Got to Be Kidding!

When we study the words, instructions, and commands of Jesus concerning how we are to love others, we soon realize there is no way we can do this on our own. He wants us to go way beyond what we can naturally do.

Jesus said, "You have heard that it was said, 'You shall love your neighbor and hate your enemy.' But I say to you, *love your enemies, bless those who curse you, do good to those who hate you, and pray for those who spitefully use you and persecute you…For if you love those who love you, what reward have you?…Therefore you shall be perfect, just as your Father in heaven is perfect*" (Matthew 5:43-44,46,48).

Again, I say, this is impossible on our own—not a chance of that happening by ourselves. But with God all things are possible. When Jesus says to be perfect the way God is perfect, He is talking about when we love others the way He does.

God's love for us doesn't mean He gives us everything we want whenever we want it. That would not be good for us. So, too, our giving to others doesn't mean giving them whatever they want whenever they want it. That is not good for them either. But how do we reconcile this with the verse that says to give whatever anyone asks of you (Matthew 5:42)?

Jesus knows we can't do this on our own, but we can love others with the *perfect love* He puts in us, and as His Spirit leads us.

Jesus also taught, "You have heard that it was said, 'An eye for an eye and a tooth for a tooth.' *But I tell you not to resist an evil person. But whoever slaps you on your right cheek, turn the other to him also. If anyone wants to sue you and take away your tunic, let him have your cloak also.* And *whoever compels you to go one mile, go with him two. Give to him who asks you, and from him who wants to borrow from you do not turn away*" (Matthew 5:38-42).

Who can do that?

Are we to allow what might be a dangerous person to hit us, or bring a lawsuit against us, or take away our clothes? If we lend to all who ask without expecting repayment, and give whatever anyone could ever ask of us, would we not soon be broke, homeless, naked, or dead?

We don't have to invite murderers and rapists into our house and give them access to our children and let them sleep in our bed, but we can pray for them to know the truth of God's Word and our heavenly Father, Jesus, and the Holy Spirit. Just praying that someone evil will come to know the Lord is a big step of love for most of us. There are people who have a calling to minister to dangerous people, and God enables them to do it. Listen to the Holy Spirit for *your* calling, and don't move into anything like this without hearing His clear direction and having it confirmed by trusted leaders.

You don't need to love *God's* enemy, who is also *your* enemy, but you do need to ask God to help you love and pray for the people who are *influenced by the enemy* and are trapped in their enemy-inspired hatred. Loving your enemy doesn't mean just someone you don't happen to like. They are not your enemy. Your real enemy is your proclaimed adversary who has planned evil toward you or those close to you.

We are in a time when certain men are spending more hours

planning ways to do more and more evil. Can our acts of love and kindness make a difference? Can our trying to be more like God in our love toward others in any way compensate for the haters of God? In certain extreme cases, probably not. But in many others, it can. It doesn't seem like it when we read of Christian churches being bombed by evil men, killing Christian men, women, and children. But we know that the death of these Christian martyrs are precious in the sight of the Lord, and they are with Him in His presence forever and rewarded for eternity.

If you are a believer and love God, how do you live around those who arrogantly disdain God and His ways? The answer is to show love for them. They don't know what to do with that. It's disarming. Love from you—that originates with the love of God within you—has power that even the firmest unbelievers cannot deny, but it still must be Holy Spirit led. You need to know what the Spirit is directing you to say and do.

One of the greatest acts of love we can give to those who hate us is our prayer that their hearts will be broken by God and softened enough to receive His love toward them.

We may never know what good we have accomplished when we pray for people who are our proclaimed enemies. But it doesn't matter. God knows.

The better we know God, the more we love Him and find ourselves developing a love for people beyond what we have had. We come to love people we don't even know because God gives us His heart for them. But sometimes it is easier to love people we don't know precisely for that reason. We don't know how irritating, selfish, and loveless they can be. We don't know how much they can hurt us.

The revelation God gave me that day He brought 1 Corinthians 13 alive to me in a new and startling way was that I was not to wait for God to *perfect me* in my ability to love others. In other words I should not *wait* to "feel it." I should *choose* to obey the commandment of Jesus to "do it."

Consistently having love for others is not only possible, it is required.

Jesus commanded it.

And He gave us His Holy Spirit to enable us to do it.

Because He gives us free will, we can *choose* to do it, remembering that what we do in love lasts forever. If we miss out on the rewards of showing love for others here on earth, we will have missed out on those rewards for eternity.

The price is too high. The consequences too final.

Prayer of *Love*

LORD, I know that without You I don't have it in me to love others the way You want me to. It's only because of Your healing and restoring love guiding me by the power of Your Spirit that I have the capacity and the strength to show love in a life-changing way. I pray You would pour Your love into my heart and give me the ability to love people the way You do. Enable me to always show love in a manner that's pleasing to You.

I pray for all believers who are persecuted for their faith. Help those of us who worship in freedom to not forget those who cannot. I don't know how much longer we will be able to worship in freedom ourselves because of evil forces everywhere who have welcomed the anti-Christ spirit into their hearts. They work day and night against those of us who love and serve You, but I hope in Your return. Help us, Your people, not to wait apathetically as if we have no input into this world. Help us to remember that our love and prayers in Your name are always more powerful than their hate.

Lord Jesus, help me to obey Your command to love others as You love me. Teach me to live in Your love in such a complete way that this is not a challenge for me but rather a way of life. Enable me to love those who are hard to love. And show me how to better express love for the ones I already love.

In Jesus' name I pray.

Words of *Love*

By this we know that we love the children of God,
when we love God and keep His commandments.

1 JOHN 5:2

Just as you want men to do to you,
you also do to them likewise.

LUKE 6:31

This commandment we have from Him:
that he who loves God must love his brother also.

1 JOHN 4:21

Above all these things put on love,
which is the bond of perfection.

COLOSSIANS 3:14

These things I command you,
that you love one another.

JOHN 15:17

16

What if I Can't Always Be Patient and Kind?

~~~~~~~~~~~~~~~~~~~~~~~~~~~~~~~~~~~~~~~

When you finish reading about all the ways God wants us to show His love for others in these next few chapters, I am sure you will see, as I do, why it's impossible to do it without His help.

First of all, we are finite and can be inconsistent and moody. We can be selfish, and at certain times the thought of denying ourselves in favor of someone else is the last thing we want to do. We can develop an attitude and carry grudges. We can dredge up unforgiveness even after we thought we had long ago dealt with an offense or injury for the last time.

We can be impatient and unkind and think of ourselves more highly than we ought. We can be negative and hopeless and not value who God made us to be as much as we should. We can be irritating in countless ways without even realizing it.

Fortunately, God understands our human limitations, so He shares His strength with us when we humbly turn to Him. What pleases God is for us to be a channel of His love to others. It is one of the ways He reveals Himself to people in the world. When we hold back and don't make it a point to love others, we hinder the spread of God's kingdom—at least as much as is up to us.

Love Is Patient

Being patient with others is an act of mercy. And you know how God feels about mercy. It's a sign of His great love. We show love and mercy when we are patient with people. It actually helps us to be patient when we remember that in the process we are expressing our love for God.

Along with love, long-suffering is a fruit of the Spirit. Only the Holy Spirit can produce this in us. We can't conjure it up on our own. When we invite the Holy Spirit in us to have full control over our lives and to work in us according to His perfect will, He produces all of the fruit of the Spirit—including patience.

Another word for "patience" is "long-suffering." The Bible says, "Love suffers long" (1 Corinthians 13:4). I love the word "long-suffering" because it says it all. It's suffering for a long time because of a person or situation.

Patience and long-suffering can be interchangeable. But in our culture today, patient is what a woman is with her husband when he forgets to pick up an important food item she requested from the grocery store on the way home from work. Long-suffering is what she is when her husband has started drinking again and she is determined to pray harder for him to find help for his problem instead of leaving him.

We have patience with a young child because we love him. We want him to learn to do the right thing, and we know he learns best in an atmosphere of love and acceptance. But if, God forbid, he grows up and becomes rebellious beyond what your patience can endure, you become long-suffering in praying for him to return to his family, his God, and his senses.

Patience is the ability to be wronged, inconvenienced, wearied, or inundated and yet still wait on God for that person or situation and not retaliate, punish, or give up.

Other words for "patient" are tolerant, forgiving, charitable, big-hearted, openhearted, sympathetic, understanding, enduring, steadfast, constant, unwavering, tireless, undiscouraged, and forbearing.

To be patient is to put up with, make the best of it, grin and bear it, and be uncomplaining. Are we always that way with everyone? Not likely.

We could take each one of those words individually and search them out to their fullest meaning, but that's not necessary. We are convicted already by just reading these. Each word points to the fact that we cannot be patient or long-suffering on our own—at least not to the extent God wants us to be—without His love poured into us by His Spirit. We need His patience poured into us.

Showing patience is not being resigned. It's joyful anticipation of what God is going to do, not only in the person with whom you are being patient, but also in you.

Sometimes we are impatient with God. We want Him to answer our prayers *now* and in the way we want them answered. But our love *for* Him has to be greater than what we want *from* Him. I've seen too many people walk away from God because He didn't answer their prayers the way they wanted Him to. They didn't love Him enough to have the patience to wait for Him to answer in *His* way and His time. I know someone who decided to become an atheist because when he prayed for a family member to be healed she died anyway. He didn't know God well enough to love Him enough.

Prayer is not telling God what to do. It is coming to Him in humility and with gratitude, which are signs of love, and sharing our heart's desire with Him—trusting He knows best.

Loving God means respecting His sovereignty and His will and the fact that *He* decides who dies and when. We do not exhibit love for God when we indict Him for not acting in accordance with our dictating prayers.

Being patient with someone is not enabling him to continue doing something that is annoying or dangerous to himself or others. We should not give up on a person's ability to get free, but we don't allow that person to keep on sinning against us, other people, himself, or God. We should not permit anyone to verbally, physically, mentally, or emotionally abuse us or anyone else. Enabling that kind of action is neither love nor patience. Getting free from such a person is not being impatient, it is wise.

How do you recognize the cutoff point for someone who continues to live in error, sin, or rebellion? When do you say "enough" to someone who is insisting on going off a cliff and you no longer want to watch, be a party to it, or go off the cliff with him? When does your patience appear to be an endorsement of the error in which that person is living?

You can only know the absolute correct answer to each of these questions by hearing the leading of the Holy Spirit. When He tells you to show tough love, you must say to that person, "I have been patient with you and this issue, but you know how I feel about what you are continuing to do. Although I love you, I cannot stand by and give the appearance that I approve in any way what you are doing. I choose to love you by praying for you to be brought to your knees before God in repentance for not living His way. I have released you into God's hands and pray He will speak to you and you will hear Him clearly."

Of course, if you are saying that to your two-year-old, be prepared for a blank stare. Come to think of it, you could get the same stare from an adult too, but at least you have established a boundary, you know your limits, and you have brought God into it.

Sometimes the most loving thing you can do for someone is to pray that they will fall into the hands of the living God and have a great awakening. Some people only learn from a hard lesson before they turn to God. You can love them by praying for that to happen and at the same time pray that the enemy will not destroy them in the process. That, too, is love.

Love Is Kind

Showing love for others means being kind, and there are countless ways to do that. One of the ways is to recognize when others need to be affirmed. In the word "praise" there is also an element of *calming, pacifying,* or *soothing* with our words. This doesn't mean we conjure up something about someone and tell them white lies to make them feel good. We tell the truth. If you cannot see anything good about a particular person, ask God to show you what *He* sees in them. The treasure chest of praiseworthy things you can find in someone is amazing when you see them from God's perspective.

The Bible instructs us to thank God for His love and kindness day and night. "It is good to give thanks to the LORD…to declare Your lovingkindness in the morning, and Your faithfulness every night" (Psalm 92:1-2). We learn about lovingkindness from God. As we praise and thank Him for His love and kindness to us, He touches and expands our heart to receive those things.

Showing kindness means not being controlling. There is a difference between love and control. We don't force people to love us, and we don't force them to receive what we want to give them. When we try to control another's emotions, thoughts, or actions, that is not love. Even God, who created us, doesn't try to control us. He loves us unconditionally, and He gives us a free will to make choices about whether to receive His love and to love Him in return. We need to allow others to do the same.

Showing kindness means reaching out to other people in ways that are evident to them. It's a choice that means sacrificing what we want to do at that moment. It's an act of love, keeping in mind that God calls us to live the life He has given us for *Him* and to bless others with His love extended through us to *them*.

Jesus didn't set us free to do whatever we want. He set us free to do whatever He wants.

Showing kindness means spending time with others in order to touch their lives.

We've all seen people who think that personally experiencing God in exciting ways is the extent of their life and giving of themselves to others is not part of experiencing God. But a large part of experiencing God is showing love and patience to others. In fact, not actively showing love to others limits the depth of our experience in God's presence.

If our life consists of only experiencing God by ourselves all alone, or even with a cherished partner, and that is the extent of it, we are greatly limiting what God wants to do in us and through us. We become self-focused thinking only about our godly experience. Yes, absolutely God wants us to experience His presence personally, but we are not to stop there. He edifies us so we can edify others.

We must be convinced that Jesus is the answer to everything while also keeping in mind that He is the answer to everything for other people as well, and they need to know that.

Jesus said that when we sacrifice of our life for Him, we will gain (Matthew 16:25). We find amazing and wonderful things in our life when we lay down our time and effort in order to show love for others. We have to love people enough to care about where they will spend eternity and where their life is headed now.

Showing kindness to others is something we should actively pursue. It means saying to the Lord, "Who can I show love and kindness to today?"

Jonathan had been David's closest friend, but Jonathan and his brothers were killed by their enemy. And their father, King Saul, also died on that same day (1 Samuel 31:1-6). After David became king, he asked, "Is there still anyone who is left of the house of Saul, that I may show him kindness for Jonathan's sake?" (2 Samuel 9:1).

David found out that Jonathan had a son named Mephibosheth (Meh-fib'-o-sheth), who had been kept alive and hidden when his family was killed. So David had him brought to his house to live.

David told Mephibosheth, "Do not fear, for *I will surely show you kindness* for Jonathan your father's sake, and will restore to you all the land of Saul your grandfather; and you shall eat bread at my table continually" (2 Samuel 9:7). David treated Jonathan's son like one of his own (2 Samuel 9:11).

David specifically asked God whom he should show kindness to. And that's what we must do as well. Ask God to show you who needs an act of kindness shown to them today and what should that be. For many people, simply a smile and a kind word of encouragement can make all the difference in their life.

When I had just moved to a different state and felt sad and lost, a stranger smiled at me and said a few kind words, and it meant more to me than I could have imagined. I never forgot it. Someone around you may need to know that you see them and they are valuable.

Other words and phrases for "kind" are benevolent, helpful, pleasant, forgiving, conciliatory, generous, not resentful, not revengeful, tolerant, friendly, amicable, peaceable, congenial, agreeable, favorable, well intentioned, well meaning, friendly, gracious, warmhearted, tenderhearted, sympathetic, charitable, considerate, compassionate, gentle, affable, and sensitive.

Is this always the way we are to everyone? Which word do we need God to work in us today?

Showing kindness means not criticizing others. We've all been around people who look for the negative in others and watch closely to find reasons to criticize them. You may be around someone like that right now. They claim they are being critical for the person's own good, but we sense their lovelessness. We feel it. It spoils the atmosphere. It's suffocating. It destroys relationships. And it not only kills others, but it brings death into the criticizer's life as well. No one wants to be in the presence of someone in whose life is a distinct lack of the flow of God's loving-kindness. That is one way to shut off the blessings of God and the depth of His presence they can experience.

Being kind means forgiving others. We can do that because God has forgiven us. "You, Lord, are good, and ready to forgive, and abundant in mercy to all those who call upon You" (Psalm 86:5).

Because we receive God's mercy and forgiveness, we can show our gratefulness to Him by extending mercy and forgiveness to others. God's love, kindness, mercy, and forgiveness are abundant toward us. He is not stingy with it. He wants us to be the same way toward others.

We won't know how God wants us to show His loving-kindness toward others unless we ask. We have to do what God asks us to do. The word *agape* is what Paul used to describe love. It's the kind of love that is a choice and not based on whether the one we love is worthy of our love. Just as we also need God's power working in us to live out our faith and stand strong in it, we also need God's love in us to love others in a way that pleases Him.

Prayer of *Love*

LORD, I ask You to fill me afresh this day with Your Spirit and Your love. Help me to develop a nature more like Yours. On my own my patience is limited, and my ability to extend love and kindness to others is imperfect at best. I know that whatever I do or say without Your love in my heart is meaningless and accomplishes nothing. Enable me to say and do everything from a heart that has been melted and molded to more resemble Yours.

I lift my heart to You and ask You to fill it with Your patience, mercy, and kindness. Show me each day who especially needs an act or word of kindness from me and what that should be. Make me sensitive to the needs of others, and give me sensitivity to Your Spirit speaking to my heart and guiding me in this. I know that patience, kindness, and love are all connected (2 Peter 1:7). There are great rewards when I extend them to other people.

Help me to be merciful and forgiving to others. Enable me to be tolerant, bighearted, understanding, steadfast, amicable, tenderhearted, considerate, sensitive, unwearied, and compassionate with other people, just as You are with me. Enable me to be patient and kind with everyone and glorify You in the process.

In Jesus' name I pray.

Words of *Love*

Love suffers long and is kind; love does not envy;
love does not parade itself, is not puffed up; does not
behave rudely, does not seek its own, is not provoked,
thinks no evil; does not rejoice in iniquity, but rejoices in
the truth; bears all things, believes all things,
hopes all things, endures all things.

1 Corinthians 13:4-7

Because Your lovingkindness is better than life, my lips
shall praise You. Thus I will bless You while I live; I will lift
up my hands in Your name.

Psalm 63:3-4

If anyone desires to come after Me, let him
deny himself, and take up his cross, and follow Me.
For whoever desires to save his life will lose it, but whoever
loses his life for My sake will find it.

Matthew 16:24-25

As the elect of God, holy and beloved, put on tender
mercies, kindness, humility, meekness, longsuffering;
bearing with one another, and forgiving one another, if
anyone has a complaint against another; even as Christ
forgave you, so you also must do. But above all these
things put on love, which is the bond of perfection.

Colossians 3:12-14

17

In What Ways
Do I Reveal a Lack of Love?

There are eight characteristics that describe what true love does *not* do (1 Corinthians 13:4-6). If you or I or anyone else exhibits any one of these traits, that will always be a glaring sign of lovelessness in us. While it's certainly easy to observe these tendencies in others, it's not always so easy to recognize them in ourselves. But we can ask God to show us the way we are and help us to be the way He wants us to be. I know that takes courage, but if we allow ourselves to be loveless, then we shut off the blessings He has for us. We have lost something everytime one of these characteristics is revealed in us. And God is not glorified or blessed by it.

Envy in Us Reveals a Lack of Love for Others

Love does not envy.

We are supposed to want the best for other people, not begrudge them for what they have. The psalmist said he was envious of the boastful and proud when he "saw the prosperity of the wicked" (Psalm 73:3). They seemed to have no problems. They even spoke against God and appeared to not only get away with it, but they continued to increase in their wealth and prosperity (Psalm 73:9,12).

He felt he kept his heart clean in vain because he suffered greatly and was often punished or disciplined (Psalm 73:13-14).

Haven't we all felt like that at one time or another? We see someone living a prosperous life, seemingly without any problems whatsoever, while we try to always do the right thing and serve God to the best of our ability, and yet we also suffer greatly, are attacked by the enemy, and face problems in many areas of our life. We don't get away with anything. We see how easy life appears to be for others and how difficult it is for us. Not that we are trying to get away with something, but if we even *thought* about doing some of the things the people who don't serve God do, we would be flattened before God in repentance and suffer immediate consequences.

The truth is, God is with us through all of our struggles and brings lasting good out of our bad situations. He disciplines us because He loves us and wants the best for us, and our life is better for it.

The psalmist continues to say he felt that way, too, until he "went into the sanctuary of God" and "understood their end" (verse 17). Once he was able to see things from *God's* perspective, he saw the punishment for people living apart from and in rebellion to Him, and it was that they would live "in slippery places," and God would "cast them down to destruction," and they would be "brought to desolation" in a moment, and be "utterly consumed with terrors" like in a bad dream, only they would not wake up from it because it would be real and for eternity (verses 18-20).

The psalmist recognized how foolish he had been to be envious of the ungodly when God was always with him, always upheld him, always guided him with counsel, and that his ultimate end was to be with the Lord forever (verses 21-24). He saw that those who live far from God will perish and receive an eternity without His presence, but he would only draw nearer to God until he was in His holy presence for eternity. The wicked will be consumed with torture and terror and unable to take their riches and charmed life with them. Why would we ever be envious of that?

Other words and phrases for "envy" are covet, desire for oneself, begrudge, feelings of being inadequate or unacceptable, rivalry, overpossessive, mean-spirited, ungenerous, or constantly comparing ourselves to others and always falling short.

These descriptions all reveal a lack of love for others and a shortage of gratitude and appreciation for who God made us to be. We can't ever let them be a part of us in any way.

For us to exemplify any one of these characteristics makes us feel and appear unattractive, self-centered, and small. And it points out the fact that we are not sold out to God because we are not trusting Him with our lives. We don't want that.

The plan of the enemy is to sow seeds of envy in your mind and take away blessings from your life.

Ask God to show you if any of these words could be used to describe you. If you see any one of these traits in yourself, confess it to God. Ask Him to help you always be happy for others when they succeed. If you find you are envious of the *godly,* trust that God gives each of His children gifts and blessings and a path to walk that keeps us in His will. When God blesses one of His children, that doesn't mean He won't bless you. God has blessings for your life as well. Make Him your priority and focus, and want what He wants for your life. Humble yourself "under the mighty hand of God, that He may exalt you in due time" (1 Peter 5:6).

When we are envious of anyone, it reveals that we don't love them. If we cannot be happy for someone's success or blessings, we need to spend more time with God thanking Him for all He has given us and basking in His love.

Flaunting Ourselves Reveals a Lack of Love for Others

Love does not parade itself.

Have you seen someone who always dresses to be the center of attention? I am not talking about trying to look nice and pleasing with good grooming and tasteful attire. I am talking about someone who silently screams, "Look at me! Look at me!" Their necklines are too low, their clothes are too tight. They are over the top. They make others feel uncomfortable to be around. I am not talking about entertainers and celebrities whose job it is to attract attention when they are working. They are paid to not be boring. Even then, some of them are way over-the-top and tasteless, but that only happens to those who are far from God.

When we always draw attention to ourselves in an obnoxious manner, it speaks of a lack of love in our hearts for others. It says, "Let's talk about me" not "How are you doing?" If we truly love others, we won't want to make them feel bad about themselves, as if by stark comparison they fall short of us.

When we dress appropriately for the occasion, it shows love and respect for other people. I am not saying to look like frump-girl because it will make people feel better about themselves. I am saying we should present ourselves in a way that glorifies God and is considerate of others.

Other words and phrases for "parading ourselves" are making a spectacle, exhibition, ostentatious, flaunt, exhibitionism, showing off, make a great show of, dangle before the eyes, and trumpet forth.

I have another definition—anything that shouts "Me! Me! Me!"

The intention of the heart is the issue here. I have erred in both directions in my life. I have been overdressed for an occasion I thought would be more dressy than it was. I should have checked on that more closely. It made me feel uncomfortable and self-conscious, and because of that I didn't put my focus on other people as much as I would normally have done.

I have also erred in the other direction and attended an event casually dressed that turned out to be a dressy occasion. I felt my casualness was an affront to the people there as if I did not think enough of their event to get dressed up for it. Again, I should have checked and not assumed something I didn't know for sure.

Whatever the situation, we need to ask God to make us sensitive to others around us so that we do not draw undesirable attention to ourselves in any way. It is the loving thing to do.

Being Prideful Reveals a Lack of Love for Others

Love is not puffed up.

Being puffed up with pride shows a tremendous lack of love for God and for others. It means we are arrogant toward God and delusional in thinking of ourselves more highly that we ought. *"Pride goes before destruction,* and a haughty spirit before a fall" (Proverbs 16:18).

Pride in any form always leads to rebellion against God. That was Lucifer's sin before he fell from heaven. He thought he could be God and take over God's world, but instead he fell from his place and his purpose. Pride will always destroy a person and their purpose. *"Do not be wise in your own eyes;* fear the LORD and depart from evil. *It will be health to your flesh,* and strength to your bones" (Proverbs 3:7-8).

Some people work hard to do right and seek God passionately in the beginning of their walk with Him, but after they establish themselves in the things of God and become successful, that can become a point of pride. This is a dangerous place to be, especially if they think they are special and God's rules no longer apply to them. God will not tolerate that, and their future will be bumpy at best. "The one who has a haughty look and a proud heart, *him I will not endure*" (Psalm 101:5). God is close to the humble but distant from the proud (Psalm 138:6). Pride reveals a lack of love.

We who truly love God will never be prideful, and we who truly love others will never be arrogant.

Other words and phrases for "puffed up" are inflated, blown out of proportion, overpraised, overrated, overemphasized, overdone, too much, excessive, go to one's head, and arrogant.

Other words and phrases for "prideful" are vain, overbearing, haughty, proud, conceited, boastful, stuck up, uppity, condescending, self-proclaimed, presumptuous, disdainful, snobbish, assumption of superiority, chief of the deadly sins, and to give oneself airs.

When the disciples asked Jesus who was the greatest in the kingdom of heaven, He said, "*Whoever humbles himself as this little child is the greatest in the kingdom of heaven*" (Matthew 18:4). A child is *humble* and *teachable* and *submissive*. The arrogant cannot even comprehend the kingdom of God, let alone dwell there, because "God resists the proud, but gives grace to the humble" (James 4:6).

Pride causes us to think, *I don't need God. I can do this myself.* That goes along with an unteachable spirit. People who think they don't need God for anything will not experience God's greatness toward them. Isn't it amazing to look at people who think they don't need God? How do they not see that they are one step away from disaster at any given moment without His protection or provision? Let's pray we can always recognize pride in ourselves and confess it immediately to the Lord. The last thing we want is a fall of any kind.

Being Rude Reveals a Lack of Love for Others

Love does not behave rudely.

When we don't display good manners and are not courteous to others, we show a distinct lack of love. Always. When we are knowingly rude and offensive to someone, we show that the love of God is not in us. If we truly have the love of God in our heart, we will be considerate because we care about and love other people.

I know a man who is often rude to his wife, even in front of other people. That embarrasses her and makes other people feel uncomfortable as well. God frowns on husbands and wives treating each other rudely. In fact, it can keep their prayers from being answered. Rudeness is a sign of arrogance. Anyone thinking they will benefit from being rude to others—especially their spouse—is deceived. God never blesses rudeness.

Other words and phrases for "rude" are harsh, gruff, cocky, disrespectful, coarse, crude, crass, raunchy, obscene, uncouth, without manners, impolite, uncivil, ungracious, heavy handed, tasteless, offensive, improper, unseemly, vulgar, and deceived.

Any of these words indicate a lack of the love of God in the heart of the person who behaves in this way. We must ask God to make us aware if we are ever like that or even tempted to be like that. Believers who are rude reveal a serious lack of maturity in the things of God. They don't understand Him or His ways at all. Their lovelessness will always limit what God wants to do in their life.

Selfishness in Us Reveals a Lack of Love for Others

Love does not seek its own.

Seeking everything for ourselves without any thought of what others need shows a distinct lack of love on our part. If we have love in our hearts for others, we will care about what blesses or helps them.

When we are constantly demanding our rights, or insisting that we have the best, or helping ourselves to the biggest and best of everything without a thought as to the needs of others around us, then we are seeking our own. Someone who always takes the best for themselves and never considers offering the best to anyone else is selfish.

Love doesn't mean never thinking about yourself. That isn't good either. It means that you think about other people besides yourself. Love is not thinking, *Me first*, and *What can I get for myself?*

Other words and phrases for "seeking its own" are self-serving, self-advancement, self-promotion, self-devotion, self-absorbed, self-driven, self-interest, personal ambition, narcissism, and wrapped up in oneself.

When we speak in such a way that makes someone else look bad while making ourselves look good, we reveal our lovelessness and God is not pleased. "Whoever secretly slanders his neighbor, him I will destroy" (Psalm 101:5). Not pleased at all.

Selfishness is all about seeking everything for yourself, such as rights, focus, attention, and material things. It's always saying, "What's in it for *me*?" "How does this promote *me*?" "How does this serve *my* interests?" "How does this make *me* look important?" "How does this serve *my* needs?"

When we don't seek our own will but seek God's will first, He fills us with His love so that we can look out for the rights and needs of others.

Being Easily Annoyed Reveals a Lack of Love for Others

Love is not provoked.

Have you ever observed someone who is easily angered, frequently irritable, offended, and touchy? They are not willing to let even the most minor incidents of what they perceive to be slights go past them. They *look* for things to be irritated about and don't stop to see if the person who has caused their anger perhaps did not intend it the way they took it. They get annoyed over nothing. In fact, they enjoy finding reasons to be upset.

This is not to say that if you ever have had any of these feelings you are a loveless person. We all can feel any of these ways at one time or another and with good reason. But for some people, acting like this has become a way of life. They secretly think they are justified in doing so. Again, the "It's all about me" syndrome is in effect.

Other words and phrases for "provoked" are annoyed, aggravated, incensed, miffed, peeved, ruffled, exasperated, bothered, harried, driven up the wall, plagued, irked, hassled, irritated, soured, vexed, and get on one's nerves.

It's up to us to see these signs of lovelessness in ourselves. If we are easily provoked, it's a sign that the love of God is not manifesting clearly in us. Yes, there are people who can be irritating or provoking, but we need to do the loving thing in the situation, whatever that may be. We must determine to overlook things people say and not be brought down by them. We will be a lot happier that way.

Ask God to teach you how to deal with irritating and loveless people. Do you mention it? Or do you quietly pray? He will show you. In the meantime, ask God to put love in your heart for the irritating, exasperating, and annoying people in your life. You know, the kind who are easily provoked.

Entertaining Bad Thoughts Reveals a Lack of Love for Others

Love thinks no evil.

People who entertain evil thoughts are usually thinking them about other people—or about doing something that will affect other people adversely. A person who thinks bad thoughts has guile. In other words, they have an insidious cunning in trying to do something hurtful through clever deception.

If we have no ulterior motives, no selfish agenda, no secret schemes or plans, or no concocting a way to serve our selfish needs at the expense of others, then that means we have no guile.

Other words for "guile" are deceit, underhandedness, duplicity, craftiness, suspicious, cunning, sneakiness, insidiousness, concealment, stealthiness, slippery, snaky, slick, calculating, tricky, foxy, shrewd, and sly.

If we love others, we don't sit around thinking about how much we don't like them, how we wish they would be removed from our lives, and what bad thing we would like to do to them. We don't keep a record of all the wrongs that have been done to us and take it out on the people who did them. We don't allow unforgiveness and revenge to be the way we operate. We get rid of resentment and let things go.

When we think evil thoughts, they show on our face and in our personality and in the way we relate to others. Others can see evil thinking in a person, even if they can't identify exactly what it is— and it makes them uncomfortable.

Jesus said, "You have heard that it was said to those of old, 'You shall not commit adultery.' But I say to you that whoever looks at a woman to lust for her has already committed adultery with her in his heart" (Matthew 5:27-28). This shows that our thoughts can have just as much sin in them as our actions. So who, then, is exempt from evil thoughts? Who among us has not thought—even for a moment—that a certain person we know of would make the world a better place if they were suddenly removed from it? When we have thoughts like that, we have to repent immediately before God and ask Him to give us a pure heart of love that is never infiltrated by evil thinking.

Celebrating Someone's Downfall Reveals a Lack of Love for Others

Love does not rejoice in iniquity, but rejoices in the truth.

This means we hate what God hates and love what He loves. He loves His truth and His people. If we are happy when an injustice happens to someone, or gleeful when we see others fail or their shortcomings revealed, or we look forward to spreading bad news about someone, we are rejoicing in iniquity. If we, instead, look forward to sharing *good* things about people and situations, and we rejoice in every manifestation of truth, and we are not happy about another's suffering or downfall, then we have love in our heart for them. If we despise inequality of treatment, or any impropriety or unlawfulness, or we have disdain for anything that should not be, and we do not celebrate evil, error, villainy, abominations, atrocity, disgrace, impropriety, transgression, trespasses, moral weakness, wickedness, unwholesomeness, or sin, then that pleases God and shows our love for Him and others.

Other words and phrases for "iniquity" are injustice, wrongfulness, what should not be, unlawfulness, illegality, wrong, error, abomination, inequity, scandal, viciousness, vileness, foulness, heinousness, criminal activity, indiscretion, dereliction, crime and reprehensibility.

Rejoicing in the truth means celebrating *God's* truth about someone, not the glaring and appalling truth you see as they manifest the way they are. It means seeing their potential and not their failure.

You recognize what *God* says about them and not what others say to disparage them.

The opposite of love is racism. It's everything Jesus is not. It goes against all that God is and does. It's evil. It's demonic at its source and in its perpetuation. It's a ploy of the enemy to steal, kill, and destroy everyone involved—the hated as well as the haters. Its cruelty comes from a dark place, "for the dark places of the earth are full of the haunts of cruelty" (Psalm 74:20). Racism is a haunt of cruelty. It perfectly sums up what celebrating evil is about. It illustrates what rejoicing in iniquity means. It's vile and evil, and perpetuators of it will pay a high and regrettable price.

All of the above characteristics of what love is *not* show us how to recognize a lack of love in our own hearts. They help us to recognize a lack of love in others as well, but for the purpose of praying for them to come to the Lord to get free.

There is a price to pay for lovelessness, but the good news is that we don't have to live this way. God can free us from all of that and keep our hearts filled with His love. But this is a choice we make. We choose to let our heart overflow with God's love, we choose to express our love for Him, and in the process our heart of love overflows to others. This is seen in the way we talk to and act toward people, and it pleases them as well as God.

Prayer of *Love*

LORD, help me to recognize anything in me that reveals a lack of love in my heart for others. Teach me to understand what love *is* by also understanding what love is *not*. Help me to never envy others, but to be happy for all that they *have* or *are*. Thank You that You have given me so much for which I am grateful. Keep me from ever flaunting, parading, or drawing attention to myself. Make me aware of the way I am presenting myself to others so that I do not make anyone feel bad but rather loved.

Help me to want what *You* want more than what *I* want. Keep me from being easily provoked, irritated, or hurt. Remove from my heart all pride. I know it can only lead to destruction because it's blatant rebellion against You. Save me from ever becoming haughty and aligning myself with the enemy. Stop me from becoming wise in my own eyes because I know You are merciful to humble people and You bring down those who are haughty (Psalm 18:27).

Give me a heart that is sensitive to others so that I am never rude or selfish. Fill my heart and mind with Your truth so that I never entertain evil thoughts. Keep me from celebrating another's bad news or downfall. Enable me to discard any offense from an irritating person so I can let it go and not carry it like a burden. Help me to love others in the way You want me to, and to reject all indications of lovelessness in me.

In Jesus' name I pray.

Words of *Love*

The backslider in heart will be filled with his own ways,
but a good man will be satisfied from above.

PROVERBS 14:14

LORD, You have heard the desire of the humble;
You will prepare their heart;
You will cause Your ear to hear.

PSALM 10:17

There is a way that seems right to a man,
but its end is the way of death.

PROVERBS 14:12

Humble yourselves under the mighty hand of God,
that He may exalt you in due time.

1 PETER 5:6

Let no one seek his own,
but each one the other's well-being.

1 CORINTHIANS 10:23-24

18

How Will Others Know I Am God's?

It must grieve God's heart to see His children fighting over small things instead of rejoicing over big things. We fight over things that divide instead of rejoicing together over the things that unite us, such as the miracle of Jesus' birth, death, and resurrection, and His unconditional love, mercy, and grace toward us.

People can't even agree on the Holy Spirit. There is probably more disagreement on that very subject in the body of Christ than any other because of two extremes—people who can't even say the words "Holy Spirit," and others who allow themselves to get crazy, scary, and weird in the name of the Holy Spirit. Is it a coincidence that those two extremes least exemplify the love of God?

Those who can barely acknowledge that the Holy Spirit exists don't allow Him to pour His peace, comfort, and love into them. They don't want Him interrupting *their* plans for *their* life. Those at the other extreme are so into *themselves* and *their experience* that the last thing they are thinking about is how to show the love of God toward others.

Both camps love their experience more than they love God. I know that may sound harsh, but I have seen these extremes a number of times in various places and, believe me, I do not sense the love of God or the presence of the Holy Spirit in either one. I sense a movement of the flesh.

The same is true for those who are loveless, self-proclaimed critics of other Christians. I am not talking about those who speak the truth into another's life because they deeply love that person and want the best for them. Don't worry if you are wondering if that is you. Those people will not be reading a book on love because the love of God is not what they are interested in. They are interested in bringing other people down and not building them up in the things of God.

A ploy of the enemy is to divide believers and pit them against one another. Imagine if we in the body of Christ were so united that we could pray in unity for whatever God put on our hearts. Think of what could be accomplished.

Love Other Believers as Jesus Loves Us

Jesus said, "A new commandment I give to you, *that you love one another; as I have loved you*…By this all will know that you are My disciples, if you have love for one another" (John 13:34-35). That means our love for other believers will be the main characteristic in us that demonstrates who it is we belong to and who we love and serve. It will be distinctive and defining when we consistently demonstrate the love of Jesus to one another.

The love of Jesus was *sacrificial* and *unconditional* and *unfailing* and not like any other love. His love in us causes us to resolve our differences and stop separating ourselves from other believers because of nitpicky issues, prickly criticism, and gossipy defamation of character that are the opposite of Christ's love for us.

Jesus wants us to bear fruit that lasts. Part of that is becoming His disciple and assisting in bringing other people to a knowledge of Him as their Savior.

We believers are all members of the body of Christ. What affects one affects us all. We all need one another. *The key is to love others as He loves us.* Love like that is not just a chance feeling. It's a choice we make that causes us to act out of love. That kind of love is something you sense in a person even if they don't do anything specifically for you. It is the way they *are.*

People will know that we are His by our love for one another. When we show love for one another by being in unity—not in allegiance to a man, but in our common allegiance to Jesus—this will draw more people to Him than anything else. This love for one another and unity of spirit require humility. That means we are not only humble before God, but humble with one another.

Our love and humility are shown in the words we speak. What we speak has to line up with what we have in our heart. When we show our love for God and for others with our words, that blesses God. *Humility is recognizing how poor we are without the Lord and how clearly pathetic our lives would be without Him.*

Paul told the Corinthians how they were to live as believers. "I plead with you, brethren, by the name of our Lord Jesus Christ, that *you all speak the same thing,* and that *there be no divisions among you,* but that *you be perfectly joined together* in the *same mind* and in the *same judgment*" (1 Corinthians 1:10).

Does that mean we all agree on everything and every detail of our lives? No, it means we agree on whom we serve as Lord and what He requires of us.

David said, "How good and how pleasant it is for brethren to dwell together in unity!" (Psalm 133:1). One of the ways we dwell in unity is to work things out together—to seek the Lord and the counsel of other strong and knowledgeable believers.

Part of loving others is being able to drop a matter. Let it go. Cut your losses and move on. We all have to do that at one time or another. Prayer is the greatest unifier of all. What could happen if we believers started praying for one another in different denominations, different cultures, and different areas so that church pride, denomination pride, and cultural and racial pride no longer existed?

Think what God could do in His people if all "we're right and everyone else is wrong" pride were eliminated.

David was set upon by false accusers who deceitfully attacked him with words of hatred. The worst part was that these were people he had loved, and they rewarded him with evil for good. But what did David do in the face of all that? He prayed. He said, "They have also surrounded me with words of hatred, and fought against me without a cause. *In return for my love they are my accusers, but I give myself to prayer*" (Psalm 109:3-4).

He prayed instead of reacting. He went to God instead of trying to get even.

What a lesson we can learn from that. Because we have the confidence of knowing God loves us, we can say, "The LORD is on my side; I will not fear. What can man do to me?...It is better to trust in the LORD than to put confidence in man" (Psalm 118:6,8). God is on your side and He knows the truth.

One of the most heartbreaking things is when a *believer* hurts you. If you both love God and He loves each of you, how do you reconcile this? You must pray for that person and for yourself. Pray that if you are wrong, God will show you. But if the other person is wrong, pray that God will reveal it to him and he will acknowledge it. The best thing would be to pray together trusting that God knows how to do what it takes to reconcile this breach.

Love Unbelievers the Way God Loves Us

Our love extended toward unbelievers will make it known to them that we don't just love our own, and that is what makes us unique. We love those who are not like us instead of rejecting them as everyone else tends to do.

The thing that keeps more people from receiving the Lord are believers who speak and act toward them without the love of God in their hearts.

That is what kept me from receiving the Lord sooner than I did.

It wasn't until I was faced with the true love of God in believers that the walls came down around my heart. Because of their prayers for me to see the light, the blindness fell from my eyes. Only God's love breaks down barriers like that. Mere human love cannot.

Pray for yourself to live in a way that the love of God can be seen in you. And pray for unbelievers to see the truth about that. Jesus said, "The world cannot hate you, but it hates Me because I testify of it that its works are evil" (John 7:7). Many people in the world hate Christians because we *are* believers in Jesus. But we must love them as well. Pray that whatever is obstructing people from seeing the truth about God's love and Jesus' sacrifice be brought down.

We forfeit all God has for us when we don't love others. Jesus said people will know us by our love for one another. But do they? Do people know that about you? Do they know that about me? I hope so. I pray so. Let's pray together that people will know us by our love for one another and also our love for those who don't know Him.

Jesus said, "Everyone who is of the truth hears My voice" (John 18:37). That means we can hear God speak to our heart because we have His Spirit of truth in us. As a result, we can be led by God in showing love to others.

Jesus said of us as believers that we will be known by our love—not by our rules and laws. Jesus did not come to judge. He came to save and set free. Our judgment on the unbelieving world has turned them off to the love of Christ because they don't see it exhibited or extended. That's a shame. We need to change that perception, one person at a time if not more. Let's pray we will be known by our love for one another as believers and for our love toward other people who do not know the Lord. Yet!

The Bible says we are to "pursue love" (1 Corinthians 14:1) and let all we do be done with love (1 Corinthians 16:14). We don't just pursue it and do it for ourselves, but for others. That's the only way people will know whose we are.

Prayer of *Love*

LORD, Your Word says that it is good and pleasant for all of us who love You to live together in unity (Psalm 133:1). And that we should love one another, for when we love You and love others, it shows that we truly *know* You (1 John 4:7). Help me to be a uniter and not a divider. Help me to be a peacemaker, a bridge maker, and a unifier.

Teach me to speak words that lift up and bring love and peace—words that edify and cause people to love You more. Enable me to speak only that which is true, righteous, and godly. Keep me from being a negative complainer. Your Word says that godly speech brings a long, good life (Psalm 34:12-13). Help me to speak the truth about what constitutes a long, good life for others. Enable me to communicate Your love to them in every way possible.

I pray I will be known for my love for You and for other people (John 13:35). I pray that even unbelievers will know me by my love expressed to them in kindness and thoughtfulness. I pray they will be attracted to You because of it. Teach me how to "pursue love"—not only to receive it, but to look to You for the opportunities You have opened to me to show it to others (1 Corinthians 14:1). Teach me how to pray to that end so I can extend Your love to those who are dividers. Enable us all to love one another with a pure heart (1 Peter 1:22).

In Jesus' name I pray.

Words of *Love*

You, brethren, have been called to liberty; only do not use liberty as an opportunity for the flesh, but through love serve one another. For all the law is fulfilled in one word, even in this: "You shall love your neighbor as yourself."

GALATIANS 5:13-14

Above all these things put on love,
which is the bond of perfection.

COLOSSIANS 3:14

May the Lord make you increase and abound in love
to one another and to all.

1 THESSALONIANS 3:12

Walk worthy of the calling with which you were called,
with all lowliness and gentleness, with longsuffering,
bearing with one another in love, endeavoring to keep
the unity of the Spirit in the bond of peace.

EPHESIANS 4:1-3

Above all things have fervent love for one another,
for "love will cover a multitude of sins."

1 PETER 4:8

19

Isn't It Selfish
to Learn to Love Myself?

〰〰〰〰〰〰〰〰〰〰〰〰〰〰〰〰〰〰〰〰〰〰〰

Most of us are way too hard on ourselves. We beat ourselves up for everything we see that disappoints us. We women, especially, are critical of ourselves. But God doesn't like that. He wants us to love the person He made us to be. He desires that we appreciate that we are wonderfully made and so we love all that our body, soul, and mind are able to do. He doesn't want us criticizing ourselves for what we think we cannot do.

I remember hearing a doctor talk about going to a foreign country to help sick children there. Many were deformed because they came from the wombs of malnourished mothers who didn't have enough to eat when they were pregnant. The next time he went to that country as a missionary, he took surgeons with him who could perform corrective procedures on the little deformed faces of those children. He said they didn't have mirrors there so they had never really seen themselves and didn't know what they looked like. They only knew the reaction of others to them. That's hard to imagine, isn't it? What would it be like to never have seen our own reflection? Most of us have been looking at ourselves in a mirror since we first saw our parents or siblings do it.

These little children were allowed to see themselves in a mirror before their surgery, and it was disturbing to them. But when they saw themselves after they were healed from their surgery, they were pleased. Their confidence and joy increased. People responded positively to them. They liked what was reflected back to them.

Too often we don't like what we see because we are critical of what we look like. We've compared ourselves to picture-perfect images we've seen in the media. But God doesn't want us to do that. He wants us to see *His* beauty in us. He wants us to see ourselves the way *He* does.

When we receive the Lord and His Spirit is in us, God begins a spiritual surgery that reconstructs and repairs all the disfiguring things that have happened to us and the damage that has occurred because of the destroying effects of sin in our life. When we see the results, we will be pleased. His Spirit in us is beautifying.

Jesus said that we should love God with all our heart, soul, mind, and strength. He said this is the first commandment (Mark 12:30). "And the second, like it, is this: '*You shall love your neighbor as yourself.*' There is no other commandment greater than these" (Mark 12:31). These are the two greatest commandments, yet how many of us do not love ourselves? In fact, we are mean to ourselves when we criticize who we think we are and don't appreciate who God made us to be.

Let me tell you a few things about you.

First of all, you were created in God's image. So were your mom and dad, and that's why you resemble them too. When you receive Jesus, *you are a new creation.* You have a new self, and from then on you must stop trying to prop up your old self.

You are the dwelling place of God's Holy Spirit and you belong to God. You were bought at a steep price, so you should glorify God in your body and spirit (1 Corinthians 6:19-20). Your body is the temple of the Holy Spirit, and that's why it should be valued and loved. Don't do anything to grieve Him—including criticizing your body, His dwelling place.

One of the greatest gifts God gives us is His Spirit living in us. We must cherish that gift and also love the temple He has given us. You have the Spirit of the one, true, living, holy God of the universe dwelling in you, so refuse to criticize yourself.

Paul said that a person should not "think of himself more highly than he ought to think, but to think soberly, as God has dealt to each one a measure of faith" (Romans 12:3). That means we don't judge ourselves on the basis of what *we* accomplish or have made *ourselves* to be, but value ourselves with regard to who *God* made us to be, what *He* is doing in us, and how *He* is enabling us to fulfill our purpose.

Stop Saying Bad Things About Yourself

We want the words we speak to always be pleasing to God, and that includes the words we say about ourselves. David prayed, "*Let the words of my mouth and the meditation of my heart be acceptable in Your sight*, O Lord, my strength and my Redeemer" (Psalm 19:14). He was talking about *all* of his words. That includes the words we say and the thoughts we have in our heart about ourselves.

If you are always beating up on yourself in the words you speak, how does that please and glorify God? How is He blessed when you criticize His creation, of which you are an important part? Paul said, "If anyone defiles the temple of God, God will destroy him. For the temple of God is holy, which temple you are" (1 Corinthians 3:17). Strong words from the One who loves you.

I used to be guilty of saying bad things about myself. Because of the terrible words my mother often spoke to me, I grew up thinking the worst about who I was. I was often told I was worthless and would never amount to anything. I was never told I had any positive attributes or that I was good at anything. I was never encouraged that I could be or do anything at all. In fact, I was discouraged and made to feel hopeless about my life.

I was not in a family of encouragers. They only ridiculed. Only one of my aunts made me feel as though I mattered in this world.

Everyone else made me feel like an imposition. So I ended up hating everything about myself and my life. I carried that self-hatred for years. It only started to heal once I received the Lord and He began to love me into wholeness. Once I was free of the self-hatred, I still felt as if I would always have to suffer for everything in life. It was never easy. It was always a struggle. And I compared my life with the lives of other people.

It took a time of healing and learning about God's love for me, and that helped me to see the truth. I saw that we all make choices every day, and when we choose to live in God's love, and choose to show our love for Him, it affects every other choice—especially *the choice to love who God made us to be.*

No one has everything. It may seem as if some people do, but they don't. So we can't set our eyes on those we think have so much more than we do and critically compare our lives with theirs.

I was extremely sick with both of my pregnancies, the second one even worse than the first. I was in bed most of the time for the second one, too sick to do anything. In the hours I spent there, I often heard the beautiful lady next door out with her perfect twin babies—a boy and a girl—that she had adopted, never having a sick or painful day at all. I allowed myself to become envious of her, comparing our situations and wanting hers and not mine. I couldn't understand why I, a believer, had to suffer so much, and she, a nonbeliever, did not have to suffer at all. I was so sick I couldn't even read or watch television. That meant I wasn't reading the Bible either. Only when a friend would come over occasionally and read it to me did I have that wonderful comfort.

After my baby was born, my neighbor brought her son over in a twin stroller to show me. Her daughter was at home. She told me that the little girl had severe disabilities, and they were going to have to move out of their home and closer to the hospital, where her daughter could receive the therapy she would need for the rest of her life. I was shocked and heartbroken for her.

After they left I cried and repented before God for my envy and lack of appreciation for what He had given me. I was extremely embarrassed that I had allowed such awful thoughts. I was embarrassed before myself and before God. It's very embarrassing to tell you this. I deeply regret my attitude of ungratefulness to God. It still pains me to think of it, and I cry about it even now. I vowed I would never again be ungrateful for what God has given me, no matter the situation. I would never again so diminish His love for me in my heart or limit my love and praise of Him. I thank God for every miserable and painful moment of my pregnancies, and I would go through it all again to have my children. I thank God every day for them. God's mercy and love toward me is beyond what I deserve and always has been.

No matter what someone else has that we think we are missing, we don't walk in their shoes. We should love them and be happy for them. And we should also love who God made us to be and the life He has given us. No matter how much we think we have suffered, there are others who have suffered more. No matter how bad we have it, there are others who have it far worse.

We have to get up every day and thank God that we woke up alive—no matter how bad we feel that day. We have to thank God for what we *can* do instead of complaining before Him about what we think we can't do. And every time we thank God for something we *can* do, let's pray for someone we know of who is unable to do what they want to do. That is loving others, and it will change our perspective on everything.

Stop Thinking Bad Thoughts About Your Life

If you find that you are constantly thinking critical thoughts about your life, ask God to help you find your hope in Him. If something needs to be changed and you have the ability to change it, do so. But if there is nothing you can do to effect a needed change, then ask God to do the impossible. Lay the situation at His feet. Ask

Him to help you see all the good things about your life and thank Him for them. Ask Him to help you see your life and your future from His perspective. Ask Him to change what needs to be changed. He is probably waiting for you to come to Him for His help. He may want the changes you want even more than you do, but He is waiting on you to depend on Him. And the reason He is doing that is because He wants to take you to places you cannot get to without Him.

God has blessings for your life you cannot even imagine right now, but He may be waiting for you to be perfected in love. That is, often God waits to bless us until we bless others in the way He wants us to—by showing love to them that comes from His heart to ours. That is one of the great blessings He gives us when we learn to love others as He wants us to. And the opposite is also true. We shut off blessings God wants to give us because we have failed to love others. This is a very big issue with Him, and too many people do not even realize it.

When you come to *truly* love and appreciate who God made you to be, you won't be filled with pride. You won't focus intensely on yourself. And you won't be envious because you don't need to be. You are you and that is good, and you don't need to be anyone else. Loving yourself and your life doesn't by any means indicate that you think you're better than anyone else. It means you appreciate the good things about yourself and the life God has given you. You realize you and your life are a work in progress, and you anticipate great things ahead. You don't compare yourself to anyone else, and you don't compare your life to anyone else's.

No matter what your past has been—you may even feel unloved, unlovable, or unwanted as I did—God sees you as valuable, with great purpose and gifts He has put in you to use for His glory. But you have to be free of the past. It does not define you today. *God* defines you. His Spirit in you defines you. Jesus defined you as being worth dying for in order to give you eternal life with Him. So do not judge yourself by your past. Yesterday is gone. Today is a new day. Just because things happened a certain way in the past doesn't mean they will happen that way today. Do not limit what God wants to do in and through you today and in the future.

You do have to forgive anyone who rejected you or made you feel unloved. Forgive yourself for not being all *you* expect yourself to be. Stop dwelling on what you think you *should* be, and start dwelling on all you *can* be in the Lord. Stop focusing on what you are not and concentrate on who you *are*. God's love liberates you to be all He created you to be. His love has set you free of your own self-imposed limits. His love *releases* you. It doesn't control you. But you have to open up to His love fully and receive it every day. When you criticize yourself instead of believing what God says about you, you are not fully receiving His love.

Each morning recognize that God has given you this day. Say, "This is the day the LORD has made. [I] will rejoice and be glad in it" (Psalm 118:24). And no matter what happens say, "This was the LORD's doing; it is marvelous in [my] eyes" (Psalm 118:23). Think of Jesus and how He was rejected, yet He fulfilled a great and magnificent purpose. "The stone which the builders rejected has become the chief cornerstone" (Psalm 118:22).

I have been rejected and am now fulfilling God's purpose for my life. If I had ended my life, as I once attempted to do and was planning again to accomplish, I would never have known what God had planned for me. The same is true for you. Don't sabotage what He is doing in your life by not loving yourself. That doesn't mean you are "in love" with yourself, which is prideful and narcissistic. Jesus said to love your neighbor as yourself. That means you must love yourself. There is a connection between loving others and loving yourself. It's healthy to love who you are—the person God made you to be—and to appreciate the life He has given you to live for Him.

His future for you is good and you will love it, just as you love Him.

Prayer of *Love*

LORD, thank You that You love me and that You made me for Your purposes. Help me to appreciate all You have put in me. Enable me to recognize the gifts You have given me to be used for Your glory. Enable me to see the good I'm not seeing and reject the self-criticism I focus on. Teach me to love You more and love myself better so I can express love to others with greater clarity.

I confess any feelings I have about my life that are negative and critical. You are in charge of my life, and I trust You to bring good into it. Give me wisdom to see the great things You have put in my life that will be used for Your glory. Help me to love others as You have taught me to love myself—that is, with great appreciation for Your work in me and in them. I know that when I love You, myself, and others that this is the fulfillment of the law (Romans 13:10). I do not want to short-circuit that in any way.

Help me to "pursue righteousness, godliness, faith, love, patience, and gentleness" because they are beautiful in Your eyes and pleasing to You (1 Timothy 6:11). Lord, You are beautiful and wonderful and lovely and attractive and desirable. Let all that You are shine through all that I am. Help me to love myself in a way that doesn't say, "I am great," but rather says, "You are great! And You are in me making me more like You every day."

In Jesus' name I pray.

Words of *Love*

He who gets wisdom loves his own soul;
he who keeps understanding will find good.

PROVERBS 19:8

Put on love, which is the bond of perfection.

COLOSSIANS 3:14

Just as you presented your members as slaves
of uncleanness, and of lawlessness leading to more
lawlessness, so now present your members as slaves
of righteousness for holiness.

ROMANS 6:19

Flee also youthful lusts; but pursue righteousness, faith,
love, peace with those who call on the Lord
out of a pure heart.

2 TIMOTHY 2:22

He who would love life and see good days,
let him refrain his tongue from evil,
and his lips from speaking deceit.

1 PETER 3:10

20

What if I'm Unable to Bear, Believe, Hope, and Endure All Things?

~~~~~~

I can't put up with this anymore." "I just can't bear it any longer." "I can't believe it's ever going to happen." "I don't believe things will ever change." "I have lost hope that this person will ever be any different." "What I have hoped for is too long in coming." "I can't endure another minute of this." "I can't keep going on this way."

Have you ever found yourself saying or thinking these kinds of thoughts about anyone or any situation? I know I have. More times than I care to admit. But that was back when I was trying to do life all in my own strength and not relying totally on God.

God is the only one who can give us the strength and stamina to bear up under the weight we are carrying. *He* is the only one who gives us the faith to believe for important things once we first believe in *Him. He* is the only one who gives us hope when we put our hope in *Him* and we put our expectations in *Him. He* is the only one who sustains us with perseverance so we can endure what we are facing.

The Bible says the kind of love we need to have is the kind that "bears all things, believes all things, hopes all things, endures all things" (1 Corinthians 13:7). But we can't do these things on our own. In fact, we were not created to do them by ourselves. Our shoulders were not built to carry this load. God knows if we have a heart that is surrendered enough to Him to rely on His help.

After Jesus was resurrected and ascended into heaven, He sent the Holy Spirit to those who believed in Him. Jesus said, "When the *Helper* comes, whom I shall send to you from the Father, *the Spirit of truth who proceeds from the Father*, He will testify of Me" (John 15:26). The Holy Spirit is our *helper* and *comforter*. He is our *counselor* and *teacher*. He helps us to do what we cannot do on our own. He is the one who enables us to bear, believe, hope, and endure all things.

Love Bears All Things

What does it mean to bear all things? It means to uphold the things *God* has called you to sustain. He has not called you to bear everyone's every burden—all your family members, friends, acquaintances, coworkers, and people you hear about. You can't do it. God doesn't want you trying to be God to other people. He—by the power of His Holy Spirit in you—will help you to bear all the things He has *called you* to do. He has not called you to be Santa Claus to everyone.

God calls us to bear one another's burdens, and one of the best ways to do this is in prayer. Heartfelt prayer that lifts the concerns of others for whom you sense a burden to pray is always God's will. We have all heard people say, *Well, all I can do is pray.* But the truth is, that is actually the *best* thing you can do. You should always start there and then do the other things He is leading you to do. When you lift up your concerns about others to God in prayer, ask Him what *He* wants you to do.

We don't need to get crazy about this. If we see a child about to run into the street where cars are driving by, we don't have to pray first to see if we should reach out and grab her. God has given us a brain, good sense, and the wisdom to make an immediate call on that.

Other words and phrases for "bear" as used in this context are suffer, put up with, overlook, lend support, maintain, sustain, uphold, undergird, bolster up, shore up, prop up, spare no effort, to go all out, endeavor to do one's best, sustain, maintain, back up, undergird the foundation of, cradle, and cushion.

Ask God to show you where you might be trying to do any of these things on your own. You may be surprised at what He shows you and how He can enable you to do it without stress.

Love Believes All Things

Believing all things means believing for the best in other people. Believing that God has a great plan for their life—and yours. Believing that God will work things out for their good—and yours. Believing that God will answer your prayers for them—and you. It means you do not *expect* the worst for others or for yourself. Nor do you *suspect* the worst in them and you are not suspicious of them.

Other words and phrases for "believe" as it is used in this context are expect, conclude, be inclined to think the best of someone, believe the best in, have confidence in, give the benefit of the doubt, give credence to, trust, assured, certainty, reliance on, acceptance, suspension of disbelief, confidence in, and sureness.

Only God can help us do all these things, especially with regard to believing for the best in people as a sign of our love for them.

Love Hopes All Things

To hope all things means we put our hope in the *Lord*. And because of that we have hope that He is working in the lives of the people for whom we pray. It means we don't give up on people and write them off. For the worst offenders, we release them to God and ask Him to work in their heart and bring them to their knees before Him. When we do that, we are assured that they have a good future ahead.

Hope is one of the three things that last, along with faith and love, "but *the greatest of these is love*" (1 Corinthians 13:13). In the end, when we are with the Lord in heaven, we will no longer need faith because faith will become sight. We will no longer need hope because all our hope will be fulfilled. But we will always have love, because God is love and we will be with Him.

Other words and phrases for "hope" are cheerful expectation, state of expectancy, anticipation, prospect, likelihood, probability, presumption, certainty, trust, put one's trust in, anticipate, envision, looking forward to, looked for, hoped for, long awaited, expected, promised, and imminent.

All this means you cheerfully expect the best in people and can predict a good future for them. It means you have reason to believe that the best is yet to come because you have prayed for them. You anticipate good things from them, and you are on the lookout for good things *in* them and *for* them.

Ask God to give you the hope in Him you need for the seemingly hopeless situations and people you see around you. He will do that by putting the lasting hope in your heart that you need.

Love Endures All Things

Before I say anything else, let's get something straight. Enduring all things does not mean you allow someone to abuse you. A woman does not allow herself to be hurt, mistreated, beaten, or damaged by her husband or potential future husband. And you do not allow anyone to violate you in any way. Ever. That is not of the Lord. It is never His will for you. And anyone who tells you otherwise is aligned with evil, and you need to remove yourself from that person immediately.

Enduring all things means you are willing to go the extra mile with someone. You are persisting in the situation, and you are summoning your most patient self to go the distance to see them through their difficult situation.

Other words and phrases for "endure" as it is used here are persevere, persist, carry on, keep on, keep trying, keep up the good work, last, continue, abide, dwell, hold on, stay the course, go the distance, prevail, last long, live to fight another day, love through, and stand the test of time.

You cannot be all things to all people. You can only be what God enables you to be for the people He puts on your heart and brings into your life.

James said, "We count them blessed who endure" (James 5:11). He is talking about enduring until the coming of the Lord. It means we don't give up and end it all. Or withdraw from loving others because of the chance they will only disappoint us. We continue to do what God is calling us to do and love others as He is leading us.

Prayer of *Love*

LORD, help me to *bear* all things when it comes to loving others. I know You will not call me to go beyond what I can bear because it is You who calls me and sustains me. Uphold me so I have strength to help others and stand with them as they go through trials. Help me to *believe* all things by suspending any disbelief I have in me regarding others. If I cannot believe for the best in them, I can believe for *Your* best for them. Help me to encourage them as You have encouraged me.

Lord, help me to *hope* all things for others because my hope for them is in You. Just as I never suspend my hope in You, help me to not lose hope in other people either. Help me to not write people off who have disappointed me or seem to never respond to the hope You have for them. I have courage because I know You will strengthen my heart because my hope is in You (Psalm 31:24).

Lord, enable me to *endure* the things You have called me to as a sign of love for others. Help me to persevere in prayer for them and encourage them to stay true to You and Your Word and the promises You have given us all. Help me to keep going and trying again after someone has rejected Your love and mine. Help me to go the distance with the ones You have instructed me to do so. I don't want to be a person who only endures for a while (Matthew 13:21). I want to stay the course with You so I can stay the course with others to whom You lead me to reveal Your love.

In Jesus' name I pray.

Words of *Love*

Consider Him who endured such hostility from sinners
against Himself, lest you become weary and
discouraged in your souls.

HEBREWS 12:3

Sanctify the Lord God in your hearts, and always be ready
to give a defense to everyone who asks you a reason for the
hope that is in you, with meekness and fear.

1 PETER 3:15

We also glory in tribulations, knowing that tribulation
produces perseverance; and perseverance, character;
and character, hope. Now hope does not disappoint,
because the love of God has been poured out in our hearts
by the Holy Spirit who was given to us.

ROMANS 5:3-5

After he had patiently endured, he obtained the promise.

HEBREWS 6:15

Whatever things you ask in prayer,
believing, you will receive.

MATTHEW 21:22

21

How Can I Show Love
in Every Situation?

~~~~~~

L ove never fails.

That's what it says in the love chapter.

But we have seen human love toward us fail. Fail to materialize. Fail to go the distance. Fail to believe for the best in us. Fail to be kind. We've seen our own love toward others fail at times too.

Only *God's* love never fails.

In order for *our* love to never fail, it needs to be established on God's love first. His love in us never fails because His Spirit of love is in us. And *He* never fails. God can't fail to be who He is. So it's *our* job to see to it that we draw close to Him every day in prayer and worship and in reading His love letter to us.

We also have to ask God to guide us in all things—especially pertaining to showing love to others. It's not that we need to ask God *if* we are to show His love. We must inquire of Him *what* the loving thing to do is in each situation and each person or group of people.

First of all, you can show love in every situation simply by asking God to help you *not* show a *lack* of love in any possible way. (Remember chapter 17 about revealing a lack of love?) In some places that alone would be a great testimony to the greatness of God, not to mention a shock to those who are not used to that.

Let the Holy Spirit Lead You to Do God's Will

Jesus said doing God's will was like food to Him (John 4:34). It must become like that for us as well. When we demonstrate our love for God by doing His will, it feeds *our* body, mind, soul, and spirit too. It edifies us in ways that nothing else can.

Not long ago I made a decision to help a friend. I knew she needed my assistance, and the Holy Spirit would not let me ignore that fact. I was exhausted from many demands and deadlines and important obligations to others I needed to be doing. So I had good reasons *not* to help. But she was alone, with no one else to assist her in her move to a new place, and I was physically and mentally able to do it. All the people who said they would help her did not show up. Who wants to help someone move, right?

I knew this would take hours and it would be exhausting—and I am not a young person. But neither is she. And it was a longer drive for me than I wanted to make alone at night at that time in my life. My list of reasons for not doing it was long.

Before the encounter I had with God in the love chapter of the Bible and He convicted me about asking Him how He wanted me to show His love to others, I would not have even asked Him about this. My mind would have already been made up. But on this day I asked the Lord what I should do—because the commitments I had made to other people had to be considered as well—and the Holy Spirit impressed *clearly* upon my heart that the loving thing would be to help her. I asked God to give me the energy, stamina, and physical ability to do what I needed to do. When I headed out in my car, I felt God with me all the way. When I got to her house, my friend was overwhelmed by all that needed to be done, but because I was being assisted by the Holy Spirit, I had great clarity on how this project could be done quickly and efficiently. And God gave me strength and a clear mind that surprised me—a rare thing for me at that time of night.

Four hours later we finished what needed to be done. The most amazing thing was that on my drive home I had more strength and energy than when I started. That was a miracle from God! I had chosen to show love according to His leading, and I felt His presence in greater measure than I had ever felt it before.

Olympic runner Eric Liddell would not run in the Olympics on a Sunday because he was a strong Christian, and he obeyed God by calling the Lord's day holy—the Sabbath, a day of rest dedicated to God. In *Chariots of Fire*, a film about his life, he said of God, "When I run I feel His pleasure." He felt God's pleasure whenever he ran because he was doing God's will, and his love for God was his priority.

I felt that same thing when I chose to show God's love over my own convenience and help a lady move. I chose to ignore the cries of my flesh saying, "I can't do this! I am too old, too tired, too pressed for time." But I came out the better for it. I found strength from the Lord—strength I absolutely did not have without His enablement. And I gained a friend for life.

God enables us to do things we could never do without Him when we choose to do them in love—the love He puts in our heart for others.

Don't Assume You Know God's Will in Every Situation

Showing love to others doesn't mean we get to play God and try to meet every person's needs. That's dangerous and definitely not God's will. My husband and I learned our lesson well about that when we were trying to help someone without the leading of the Holy Spirit. We thought, *It's always good to help someone in need, right?* We cannot always make a judgment as to what a person's actual need is without knowing the facts. And only God knows the whole story.

One time we helped out someone by giving him money to pay his mortgage that month because it was way overdue and he did not have the money. It turned out that we should have given the money to his wife because he used it to buy drugs. We didn't even know he was using drugs. But she did, and she would have told us if we had asked. But we didn't seek God about it. We didn't pray first. We didn't ask questions. We *assumed* God would want us to do this. But we were *dead wrong*.

When his wife later told us what happened, we were shocked and grieved. That man later learned a hard lesson—a fall that needed to happen in order to bring him to his senses and get help—a fall we delayed for at least a month because we *enabled* him to keep his destructive lifestyle going.

We were *playing God* instead of *seeking God*.

Sometimes the most loving thing is the hardest to do. That's because what may seem to you is the best thing may actually *not* be the best for that person at that time. The money we gave would have been better used to get that man some help. We absolutely must be led by the Holy Spirit in every situation.

God decides *who. He* decides *when. He* decides *how.* We don't. That's why we need to ask Him for His leading. We are not supposed to try and be someone's savior and rush in to meet their every need so that they never have to seek God for anything. When we do that, we rob them of knowing God as their Provider, Protector, and Deliverer.

We must always remain God's instrument and remember that we work for His family business. We don't run things. We don't go off on our own trying to rescue and fix everyone. We cannot do that anyway. We don't have supernatural power and unlimited resources without the Lord. And He only lets us partake of those according to *His will* and not our own.

In a nutshell, God loves us. But we *choose to open up to His love* in order to fully *receive* it. Those who do not acknowledge God as the Father, the Son, and the Holy Spirit—all personifications of His love for us—cannot receive it. But once we do receive God's love and walk with Him, *we become overwhelmed with our love for Him.*

In our expressions of love for Him, He fills us with more of His divine nature. *The more we become partakers of His divine nature*, the more we sow seeds of His love into others, *according to His leading*. The rewards are great when we love others because then our path will be "like the shining sun, that shines ever brighter unto the perfect day" (Proverbs 4:18).

Our love for others is not manifested in order to attract people to ourselves; it is to attract them to God. And that is where this ultimately should lead. You love people enough to care about where they spend eternity. You love them enough to not want them to spend eternity forever separated from God.

God warns us in His Word that the day of reckoning will come. And we see that all signs indicate the world is quickly headed in that direction now. The day and time have been extended to give people the opportunity to make the right choice as to what side they are on. We will either choose God or His enemy during our lifetime. And by not making any choice at all, we have chosen the enemy.

Going to heaven to dwell in eternity with the one true God is only secured by people who make the choice to receive the only One who has paid the price for us in order to secure our place in heaven and have our name written in the Lamb's Book of Life. We must love others enough to help them to make the right decision.

Paul said, "Do you not know that those who run in a race all run, but one receives the prize? Run in such a way that you may obtain it. And everyone who competes for the prize is temperate in all things. Now they do it to obtain a perishable crown, but we for an imperishable crown" (1 Corinthians 9:24-25).

Run it to win it.

Showing love to another person means we are not to withhold good from those to whom it is due when it is in our power to give it (Proverbs 3:27). "Do not say to your neighbor, 'Go, and come back, and tomorrow I will give it,' when you have it with you" (Proverbs 3:28). It means we are to show love in every situation because we *have it*. When the Lord opens up an opportunity to tell some-one the reason for the hope within you, do it in love. Take the time to look that person in the eye and smile. Let them know you see them—and that they are not invisible to you, they are valuable. And you will reap blessings on earth and rewards in heaven that will last for eternity.

Prayer of *Love*

LORD, I pursue love just as I pursue You. Fill my heart so full of Your love that it overflows to others. Enable me to show Your love in every situation. I depend on You for guidance with that. Lead me by Your Holy Spirit to make decisions regarding what is always pleasing to You. I don't want to interfere with what You are doing in another's life. I don't want to move in the flesh, but instead be led by Your Spirit in all I do and say.

Teach me to not only love others with my words but also with my actions. When someone I know has experienced loss, help me to not only pray for them but do something to help them recover. I know there is a time for grief and we should not interfere with that, but when grief becomes prolonged to the point of physical and emotional paralysis, I pray You would enable me to help that person walk through it and get to the other side.

Teach me to love others with the love in my heart that comes from You. I know that "the mouth of the righteous brings forth wisdom" and "the lips of the righteous know what is acceptable" (Proverbs 10:31-32). Help me to know words that are wise and acceptable all the time. I know that "in the multitude of words sin is not lacking, but he who restrains his lips is wise," so make my words to be valuable and edifying to others and never meaningless (Proverbs 10:19-20). I know that can only happen by Your Spirit of love working in and through me.

In Jesus' name I pray.

Words of *Love*

May our Lord Jesus Christ Himself, and our God
and Father, who has loved us and given us everlasting
consolation and good hope by grace, comfort your hearts
and establish you in every good word and work.

2 THESSALONIANS 2:16-17

The ways of man are before the eyes of the LORD,
and He ponders all his paths.

PROVERBS 5:21

God has not given us a spirit of fear,
but of power and of love and of a sound mind.

2 TIMOTHY 1:7

My love be with you all in Christ Jesus.

1 CORINTHIANS 16:24

Now abide faith, hope, love, these three;
but the greatest of these is love.

1 CORINTHIANS 13:13

"When you clearly recognize His voice speaking to your heart, your life will never be the same."

God's Holy Spirit is as close as your next breath—what an amazing gift. How comforting to be able to walk in the power and presence of the Holy Spirit in every area of your life.

Beloved author Stormie Omartian has written books on prayer that have been read by millions. Now she focuses on the Holy Spirit and how He wants you to hear His gentle leading when He speaks to your heart, soul, and spirit. How He wants to help you enter into the relationship with God you yearn for, the wholeness and freedom God has for you, and the fulfillment of God's promises to you. How He *wants* to lead you to

- be transformed in your emotions and character
- discern God's guidance, blessings, and protection
- receive the inheritance laid up for you as God's child
- live out God's will for your life
- have a life that you cannot possibly live without Him

As you trust in the Holy Spirit and His great love for you, you will be filled with His mind, knowledge, and wisdom. You will grasp a vision for the special calling on your life, and you will sense His guidance in the way you should go.

"As prayer warriors, we must remember that no matter how hopeless a situation may appear to us, God gives us power in prayer to do something about it. We may be overwhelmed by it, but God is not. We may not see a way out, but God can. Because of Him, we can make a difference!"

—Stormie Omartian

Do you want a meaningful prayer life that is more than just asking for blessings? Stormie shows you how to pray with strength and purpose—resulting in great victory that advances God's kingdom and glory.

You will find help and encouragement for your own prayer life as you grow to

- know your Commander and stand on His side
- be certain of your authority in prayer
- become skilled with your spiritual weapons
- follow God's orders to resist the enemy
- see what is happening from God's perspective

If you have a heart of compassion and a desire to make a difference through prayer, simply start by saying, "Lord, use me as Your prayer warrior," and the Holy Spirit will lead you from there.

"Being a prayer warrior is something you do because you love the Lord and want to serve Him."

To learn more about Harvest House books and
to read sample chapters, visit our website:

www.harvesthousepublishers.com

HARVEST HOUSE PUBLISHERS
EUGENE, OREGON